A BEAST THAT

The peaceful residents in Dunnville, in Casey Cour. exercised and nonplussed by the appearance of a strange and destructive animal in their neighborhood, and which, for the want of a better appellation, they term "the dog-eater." Some three years ago the people of the west end of this county were the victims of the depredations of a similar animal, and the name of "the dog-eater" was given it because it preyed upon the canine tribe exclusively, and seemingly having an appetite for no other game. He suddenly disappeared from that section, however, much to the relief of the inhabitants and the local newspapers, and it was hoped that his absence would be permanent. But the animal is now creating the furore in Casey County, which is comparatively only a short distance from the scene of the former trouble, must be the original "dog-eater." The first indication of his return was last Tuesday night, or Wednesday morning rather, when Mr. G. R. Williams, who owns a large pack of fox hounds, went out to where the dogs had been chained the night before and found every one of them stark dead. There was very little evidence of a struggle, and for quite a while Mr. Williams could form no idea of the manner in which his dogs met their death.

After a second and more careful examination he found that each dog had a small wound in the throat, and he soon saw that whatever did the work overpowered the poor brutes with very little difficulty, and then perforating their throats, sucked their life blood.

COWBOYS & DOGMEN

SKINWALKERS, WEREWOLVES, AND
HELLHOUNDS OF NORTH AMERICA

John LeMay

Bicep Books
Roswell, NM

© COPYRIGHT 2022 by John LeMay.

All rights reserved. No portion of this book may be reproduced in any form without permission from the publisher, except as permitted by U.S. copyright law.

First Edition

LeMay, John.
   Cowboys and Dogmen: Skinwalkers, Werewolves, and Hellhounds of North America
      1. History—Pioneer Era. 2. Supernatural
      3. Folklore, Early Twentieth Century.

FOR DR. JOHN AND
THE SCARYCAST CREW

CONTENTS

INTRODUCTION   9

CHAPTERS
1. BRIDE OF THE WEREWOLF   17
2. DOGMAN BEGINS   23
3. BEAST OF THE LAND BETWEEN LAKES   27
4. WOLFMAN OF VERSAILLES   35
5. MYSTERY OF THE DOG EATER   39
6. PLAGUE OF THE SKINWALKERS   55
7. HELL DOGS OF ELDORADO   71
8. WATROUS WEREWOLF   81
9. BEFORE BRAY ROAD   87
10. WEREWOLVES OF INDIANA   95
11. CRIMSON COYOTE   101
12. CURSE OF THE CAT PEOPLE   107
13. THE BEAR MAN   111
14. WEREWOLF WOMAN OF TALBOT COUNTY   115
15. SAGA OF THE SHUNKA WARAK'IN   121
16. HOUNDS OF HEAVEN AND HELL   129
17. LOBO GIRL OF DEVIL RIVER   135
18. RATON'S WERERAT   143
19. BURIAL GROUND BEAST   147
20. CASE OF THE WERE-ONZA   155
21. WHAT WAS THE WAHHOO?   165
22. RETURN OF THE DOG EATER   185

POSTSCRIPT:
THE ORIGINS OF SKINWALKER RANCH   191

INDEX 204
ABOUT THE AUTHOR 206

INTRODUCTION:
THE HISTORICAL WEREWOLF

I guess I shouldn't be surprised that I'm writing a book about werewolves. As a kid, one of my all-time favorite non-fiction titles was Daniel Cohen's *Werewolves*.[1] The book shocked me for two reasons. The first was that werewolves might actually be real, and the second was that real-life werewolves were nothing like their movie counterparts.

The concept of someone becoming a werewolf due to a werewolf bite, for instance, comes from film, not folklore. Nor were werewolves native to medieval Europe, and tales of were-creatures of all kinds have been common the world over since time immemorial. Since the technical term for someone turning into a werewolf is lycanthropy, we will start our history in ancient Greece with King Lycaon.

---

[1] Cohen was quite proficient when it came to books aimed at younger readers regarding cryptozoology, ufology, and the supernatural.

LYCAON TRANSFORMED INTO A WOLF.

According to legend, Lycaon was the king of Arcadia and was turned into a wolf as punishment by Zeus or Jupiter, depending upon which version of the myth you hear. According to one version of the tale, Jupiter had recently come down to Earth and Lycaon assumed he was an impostor. To test him, Lycaon held a feast in Jupiter's honor where he served human flesh. Jupiter passed the test by declining the human meat, and also punished Lycaon by turning him into a wolf, hence the term Lycanthropy.

Yet more tales from Arcadia tell of men becoming wolves if they consumed human flesh under specific circumstances. Another more elaborate legend told of a ritual that occurred once per year wherein a man of the Anthus Clan would go out to a certain marsh. As he swam naked through the marsh, he would turn into a wolf for nine years. If, during this time, he refrained from feasting on human flesh, he could return to his human state.

Before that, Herodotus wrote of a tribe northeast of Scythia called the Neuri, which could transform into wolves once a year for several days before returning to human form. The legend was also recounted by Pomponius Mela. The great poet Virgil, in his work *Eclogues*, claimed that a man nemed Moeris used herbs and poisons picked in Pontus to transform into a wolf. One of the first Christian accounts of a werewolf can be found in Augustine of Hippo's *The City of God* and attributes witchcraft to the transformation of man into wolf.

Back then, it was believed that most any witch or sorcerer could transform into an animal, which goes against the typical Hollywood fairytale that someone must be bitten by a werewolf to change. For instance, in 1521, a man accused of witchcraft, Pierre Bourgot, eventually confessed to being a werewolf while on trial. Bourgot claimed his journey into lycanthropy began one day when he was out looking for his lost sheep. On his search, he encountered three mysterious men riding on black horses. As if by magic, they helped him locate his misplaced flock, and Bourgot kissed the leader's ring in thanks.

As it turned out, the three were emissaries of the devil, and kissing the leader's ice-cold, corpse-like hand was Bourgot's way of selling his soul. Eventually, Bourgot attended a gathering of witches where he smeared his body in a magical salve that turned him into a wolf. And with that, the shepherd who once protected his flock from the wolves became a wolf himself. Or at least, he claimed he did. Whether he took the form of a wolf or not, he killed several children, hence the reason he was on trial. Bourgot was one of many self-proclaimed werewolves of the era.

WOODCUT OF A WEREWOLF ATTACK BY LUCAS CRANACH DER ÄLTERE, 1512.

SKINWALKERS, WEREWOLVES, AND HELLHOUNDS OF NORTH AMERICA

A significant number of people were accused of being werewolves in witch trials in 16th Century France. In many cases, the accused were cannibals and there was no proof that they turned into animals, even if there was evidence that they had committed murder and consumed human flesh. Despite the lack of proof for any actual lycanthropy, there was one indisputable case where a wolf-like monster terrorized France. Of course, I am speaking of the Beast of Gévaudan. Located in what is now Lozère in south-central France, the area was originally called Gévaudan. There, eighty people were killed by a wolf-like creature over the course of three years between 1764 to 1767. Actually, eighty people is a conservative estimate. Others claim the number of victims soared into the hundreds. However many people it killed, the creature sounded more like a canine cryptid than a supernatural werewolf, as it appeared to be some kind of large wolf/hyena hybrid.

Belief in werewolves continued and was particularly widespread in medieval Europe, so much so that they were even mentioned in Medieval law codes. In King Cnut's *Ecclesiastical Ordinances*, it was written that the codes aimed to ensure that "...the madly audacious werewolf do not too widely devastate, nor bite too many of the spiritual flock." Other scholars of the time to believe in werewolves included Gervase of Tilbury, who wrote in one of this works that "...in England we have often seen men change into wolves."

The word werewolf, or specifically, in this case, "werwolf," comes from Germany. It was first recorded by Burchard von Worms in the 11th Century. For the Germans, traditions of were-beings dated back to the Scandinavian Viking Age. Harald I of Norway was said to have a group of "wolf-coated men" (Úlfhednar) in his service. The Úlfhednar were comparable to the berserkers, who wore bearskins and used the spirit of the animal for strength in battle.

Just as old women were sometimes profiled as witches for having old-age ailments, many people were likewise accused of being werewolves for their physical traits. For instance, a person who had what we would today call a uni-brow, or bushy eyebrows that conjoin, could be accused of being a werewolf. Having unruly, curved fingernails, lots of body hair, and even low-set ears could get someone accused of being a werewolf. In wolf form itself, the accused would not look like Lon Chaney Jr.'s Wolf Man. Instead, it would be indistinguishable from an ordinary wolf apart from three distinct features: the wolf possessed no tail and retained its human eyes and voice.

As I've alluded to several times now, none of the ancient records—that I know of at least—attribute becoming a werewolf to a bite. In nearly every case, some occult ritual was required, typically stripping naked and wearing the pelt of the animal that one desired to transform into. In the absence of a full pelt, a belt made of the animal hide would suffice. Other cases spoke of the accused rubbing their bodies with magical salves to induce the transformation. The most fairy-tale-like belief of all went that if one drank rainwater from the paw-print of a wolf, they could then transform into a wolf. Lastly, there was the belief that if one slept outside under the full moon on a summer night, specifically Wednesday or Friday, they could turn into a wolf. This, as far as I can tell, is where the werewolf's correlation to the full moon sprang from in fiction.

To cure someone of lycanthropy, wolfsbane could be used, while Arabic folklore claimed that striking the afflicted on the forehead with a knife would help. Exorcism was also recommended. Piercing the werewolf's hands with nails might also work. The most interesting method, though, is that one could negate the creature's supernatural power by uttering its Christian name three times. Fascinatingly enough, this also applies to the Native American skinwalker legend, where uttering the skinwalker's real name can render it powerless.

There was also an interesting belief among the Greeks in the late 1800s that the corpse of an accused werewolf had to be destroyed. Otherwise, it may rise from the grave as a wolf or hyena, which would specifically roam war-torn battlefields to drink the blood of dying soldiers.

Someone who died in an act of mortal sin was thought to return as a werewolf that drank blood at night. They were dealt with by a combined act of decapitation and exorcism. After the beheading, the head would be tossed into a river where it would sink under the weight of its sins. The same method could be used on vampires. Actually, in Bulgaria, the werewolf and the vampire were interchangeable and were collectively known as the vulkodlak.

There is also an odd association between werewolves and the number seven. In Latin America, in some areas, it is believed that the seventh son of a large family may become a werewolf. In Hungarian folklore, there was a belief that a cursed child may become a werewolf upon its seventh birthday. There is also the strange superstition that a child born on Christmas Day may become a werewolf, which was utilized in Hammer's *Curse of the Werewolf*.

In North America, werewolf tales were brought by various European settlers to our shores from across the Atlantic. As such, many of the tales recounted in this book will bring to mind the myths we've just covered as opposed to the monster movies you are no doubt accustomed to. However, this shouldn't come as a letdown. As the old saying goes, truth is stranger than fiction.

CHAPTER 1
BRIDE OF THE WEREWOLF

Though you may not associate Detroit, Michigan, with werewolves today, you have to remember that the area was settled by French fur trappers long ago. Of all the European immigrants to come to America, it was the French, more so than any other, that told tales of the werewolf, or the *loup garou* as they called it.

Most of these tales center on Lake St. Clair, named because it was discovered on the feast day of St. Clare of Assisi by a French explorer. The story we are about to discuss originated in the very late 1600s and is well known in the area.

The tale's heroine was a young woman named Genevieve Parent, who lived with her father along the shores of Lake St. Clair. Genevieve was planning to join a convent in Three Rivers, Canada. The only problem was that she had an unwanted admirer by the name of Jacques Morand. Charles Skinner related the tale in his seminal 1896 book *Myths and Legends of Our Own Land* in a chapter entitled "Were-Wolves of Detroit":

> Jacques Morand, the *coureur de bois*, was in love with Genevieve Parent, but she disliked him and wished only to serve the church. Courting having proved of no avail, he resolved on force when she had decided to enter a convent, and he went to one of the witches, who served as devil's agent, to sell his soul. The witch accepted the slight commodity and paid for it with a grant of power to change from a man's form to that of a were-wolf, or *loup garou*, that he might the easier bear away his victim.[2]

One night, as Genevieve walked along the shores of the lake, Morand, in his wolf form, took to following her. When Genevieve saw that she was being stalked by a wolf, she fled to an altar to the Virgin that she had set up along the shores at a point known as Grosse Pointe. As she fell to her knees to pray, the werewolf leaped upon her. However, the werewolf never landed and instead turned to stone. According to folklore, one of the large rock formations along the lake shore is really the stone werewolf.[3]

---

[2] Skinner, *Myths and Legends of Our Own Land*, pp.138-140 [Fifth Edition].
[3] Another folk tale alleged that back in the 1920s there was a werewolf statue housed on a farm on the lakeshore which

SKINWALKERS, WEREWOLVES, AND HELLHOUNDS OF NORTH AMERICA

WEREWOLF ATTACKING ITS VICTIM.

While the above story is certainly just a myth, contrary to most myths, the characters in the story appear to be real, as biographical information on them is readily available in the historical record. For instance, it is known that Jacques Morand came to New France (as the area was then known) with French soldier and explorer Daniel Greysolon. Morand was one of 50 men who founded Fort St. Joseph near Port Huron in 1686. This was done to prevent English traders from operating from the upper lakes. It also appears that the entire Parent family were real people who lived along the lake. How and why did they get one of the best-known werewolf legends of the Americas attached to them? We may never know, but this

---

brought about bad luck to the crops until it was tossed into the lake, and the next year's harvest was successful.

oddly isn't the only werewolf legend to hail from the shores of Lake St. Clair.

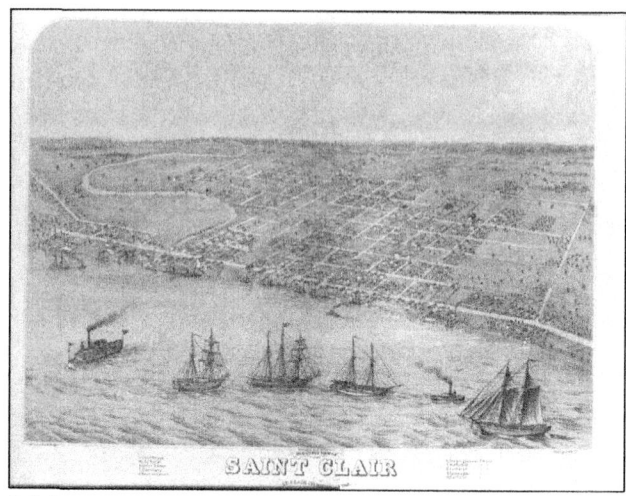

POSTCARD DEPICTING LAKE ST. CLAIR IN THE LATE 1860s.

Skinner's *Myths and Legends of Our Own Land* tells of another tale of unwanted werewolf affections in the same area:

> Harder was the fate of another maiden, Archange Simonet, for she was seized by a werewolf at this place and hurried away while dancing at her own wedding. The bridegroom devoted his life to the search for her, and finally lost his reason, but he prosecuted the hunt so vengefully and shrewdly that he always found assistance. One of the neighbors cut off the wolf's tail with a silver bullet, the appendage being for many years preserved by the Indians.

SKINWALKERS, WEREWOLVES, AND HELLHOUNDS OF NORTH AMERICA

> *Myths and Legends of Our Own Lands* had one other Michigan-based werewolf tale to offer from the same area:
>
> The man-wolf dared as much for gain as for love. On the night that Jean Chiquot got the Indians drunk and tore off their beaver skins, the wood witches, known as the "the white women," fell upon him and tore a part of his treasure from him, while a werewolf pounced so hard on his back that he lost more. He drove the creatures to a little distance, but was glad to be safe inside of the fort again, though the officers laughed at him and called him a coward. When they went back over the route with him they were astonished to find the grass scorched where the women had fled before him, and little springs in the turf showed where they had been swallowed up. Sulfur-water was bubbling from the spot where the wolf dived into the earth when the trader's rosary fell out of his jacket. Belle Fontaine, the spot was called, long afterward.

The lover finally came upon the creature and chased it to the shore, where its footprint is still seen in one of the bowlders [sic], but it leaped into the water and disappeared. In his crazy fancy the lover declared that it had jumped down the throat of a catfish, and that is why the French Canadians have a prejudice against catfish as an article of diet.[4]

---

[4] Ibid.

COWBOYS & DOGMEN

While that ending is a bit silly, a more realistic version of the tale said that the hunter tracked the wolf down to its lair and killed it, then tore up the body and fed it to the catfish. According to local lore, the boulder with the footprint on the St. Clair shore mysteriously transported itself to the corners of Chalfonte and Kerby Roads. Supposedly if you study it, you can still see the footprint of the Werewolf of Lake St. Clair.

Sources:

Skinner, Charles M. *Myths and Legends of Our Own Land.* J.B. Lippincott Company, 1896. [Fifth Edition].

Warnes, Kathy. "Genevieve, the Stone Loupe Garou, and Tonnancour: a Legend of Lake St. Clair." Meandering Michigan History.
https://meanderingmichiganhistory.weebly.com/genevieve-the-stone-loupe-garou-and-tonnancour-a-legend-of-lake-st-clair.html

CHAPTER 2
DOGMAN BEGINS

The Michigan Dogman is one of the newer cryptids, relatively speaking, to rear its ugly head into the world. Like the Lizard Man of South Carolina, the Dogman debuted into the public consciousness in 1987. And also like the Lizard Man, unbeknown to most, the Dogman had actually been sighted one hundred years earlier.

In 1887, in Wexford County, Michigan, several bored lumberjacks sighted what looked to be a normal dog. For reasons unknown, they began to chase it. The dog ran away and hid within an old, hollowed-out log. One of the loggers grabbed a stick and began poking it into the log, trying to get the dog to come out. Suddenly, the dog let out an "unearthly scream" and then crawled out of the log and stood on its hind legs. "There face-to-face and eye-to-eye with the men stood a creature with a man's body and a dog's head. The terrified men broke camp and never returned to the area," wrote Julie Royce in her book *Traveling Michigan's Sunset Coast*.

Ten years later, in 1897, came another Dogman incident in the vicinity of Buckley, where a dead farmer was found slumped over his plow. It was thought that the man was frightened to death, for in a circle around the body were the tracks of a huge dog in the dirt, as though it had been circling the man.

In 1907 came the next in what was to become an annual Dogman incident once per decade. Royce relates, "Exactly a decade later there was a report of a demented widow who reported weird dreams with dogs circling her house at night. These dogs walked like men and yelled like banshees."

In 1917, a local sheriff found an old abandoned wagon. Like the dead farmer twenty years before, in this case the deserted wagon was encircled by huge dog prints in the dusty earth. Creepier still, nearby, four horses were found dead, their eyes wide open. A local vet could find no logical reason for the horses' deaths. It was truly a mystery. No records could be found for a 1927 incident, but there was another in 1937, where a boat captain and several of his crew saw a pack of wild dogs roaming Bowers Harbor.

Royce relates another encounter that year:

> That same year, or possibly the next, Robert Fortney picked up his shotgun and killed one of

a pack of dogs that lunged at him as he stood on the banks of the Muskegon River. One dog did not run off in fright. Instead it reared up on its hind legs and glared at Fortney with slanted, yellow eyes. Fortney was unsure what to call the animal that locked eyes with him.[5]

Over the decades, the sightings would continue, and only during the seventh year of the decade. Why seven? Who knows, but we shouldn't forget the odd correlation between werewolves and the number seven, as addressed in this book's introduction.

While the number of Dogman accounts that have been unearthed after its 1987 "sighting" are remarkable, what's even more unbelievable is that the 1987 Dogman furor was just an April Fool's hoax. In fact, it wasn't even a sighting. For 1987's April Fool's Day, disc jockey Steve Cook at WTCM-FM in Traverse City, Michigan, recorded a song about a monster called the Dogman (though the song itself was simply titled "The Legend"). The only truth to the song, by Cook's own admission, was that it was based upon folklore. "I made it up completely from my own imagination as an April Fools' prank for the radio and stumbled my way to a legend that goes back all the way to Native American times," Cook told Skeptoid.[6]

---

[5] Ibid, p.419.
[6] Hudson, Alison "Wag the Dogman". Skeptoid #477. (July 28, 2015).

SCREENGRAB FROM NEWSCAST ON DOGMAN.

Ironically, as the hit song played on the local radio, it inadvertently drew out a dearth of real Dogman sightings from listeners, which continue on to this day.

Sources:

Hudson, Alison "Wag the Dogman". Skeptoid #477. (July 28, 2015).

Royce, Julie Albrecht. *Traveling Michigan's Sunset Coast.* Dog Ear Publishing, 2007.

CHAPTER 3
BEAST OF THE LAND BETWEEN LAKES

Of all the states in the U.S. to host werewolf legends, Kentucky has several to choose from, but we'll begin with the early 1800s era story of Nils Wills from the Red River Gorge area. Supposedly, Wills was the first settler in that area of Kentucky and, in the process, befriended several Cherokee hunters. While Wills was out hunting one day, he suffered a terrible accident. Atop a high cliff, he stumbled and fell to what should have been his death. Instead, he was found dying by some of his Cherokee friends.

They brought him back to their tribe and asked the tribal elders if they could help. The elders knew of only one method, something called the "Wolf Gift"—a strange ritual the details of which we do not know.

WEREWOLF ENGRAVING.

Wills awoke alive and well the next morning. More than that, his wounds had completely healed. But like all good fairy tales, this gift came with a terrible curse. From that day forward, Wills was essentially a Cherokee version of a skinwalker called a *Limikin*. However, unlike most Native American skinwalkers, which induce their transformation willingly, the *Limikin* changed from man into wolf involuntarily. Holding the Christian view of the evil werewolf, Wills was mortified. More than that, he was enraged. The Cherokee didn't understand—to them, it was a gift—but to Wills, it was a curse. He made it his mission to kill all of the tribal elders and members who had inflicted this evil upon him. After they were dead, he even hunted down their families. Allegedly Wills killed any Native American he came into contact with until his death in 1810. Or, presumed death, I should say. To this day, when hikers go missing—or half-eaten human remains are discovered—the Wills Werewolf is still blamed.

As recently as November of 2015, something akin to the Wills Werewolf was spotted in Red River Gorge by campers. The beast was never clearly seen and the witness observed only two red eyes. The devil in the details applies to the noises the creature made, which the witness said sounded like "a large man being slaughtered combined with a wolf."[7]

Leaving the Wills Werewolf behind in Red River Gorge, we will now travel to another uniquely named location: The Land Between Lakes. The area is so named because it is located between two large lakes, those being Lake Barkley and Kentucky Lake. It has been the haunt of a seven-foot-tall werewolf known as the Beast of the Land Between Lakes for generations. There are two iterations of the legend, one European and the other Native American. The European legend goes that an immigrant family from Europe came to America in the early 1800s to settle in the land "Between the Rivers." This man supposedly carried a genetic disease that he had also passed down to his children. This mysterious condition caused the family to "go mad" after nightfall. The family secluded themselves from the rest of the

---

[7] http://www.kentuckybigfoot.com/counties/powell.htm

world and the children never went to school. Many years later, in the 1900s, their homestead was found abandoned (or, in other words, there were no dead bodies). Where they went is a mystery, but some think that collectively they are the mysterious "Beast of the Land Between Lakes."

VINTAGE LAKE KENTUCKY POSTCARD.

As for the other legend, it centers around a Chickasaw shaman who could shapeshift into a wolf. He was accused by his fellow tribesmen of using his powers for evil and cast out into the wilderness. But even that wasn't enough. Some of his tribe felt he should be killed. When not enough Chickasaw agreed to help hunt down their old shaman, the willing tribesmen uncharacteristically solicited help from drunken Anglo settlers within a nearby saloon.

The combined group went out into the wild and shot the shaman in wolf form. In his dying moments, he cursed the men and vowed to return to torment them. And, sure enough, soon after, strange howls emanated from the woods, hunters mysteriously disappeared, and bison were mutilated by some hideous predator. Stranger still, livestock was occasionally discovered killed but not eaten—uncharacteristic of a predator. A few times animals were found with their legs torn from the sockets, something else a natural, known predator wouldn't have the strength to accomplish.

Eventually, settlers caught a glimpse of the strange creature, which resembled a wolf walking upright on two legs. Tales spread of families huddling within their cabins in fear as they listened to the creature walk across their porch. The next morning they would find deep gouges—claw marks—in the wood.

One old-timer claimed that it jumped out of one of the horse stalls in front of him one night, causing him to "wet his overalls".[8] Another old-timer and

---

[8] https://mysteriousuniverse.org/2017/08/the-bizarre-beast-of-the-land-between-the-lakes/

his wife claimed to see it get tangled in chicken wire while trying to get into their chicken coop. Other stories are not so humorous, though. A more recent one from the 1980s claims that a murdered family was found within their camper. Well, the parents were found in their camper; the child was found half-eaten high up in a tree. Of course, if you're wondering why you didn't hear this sensational story in the news at the time, it was supposedly covered up by the local government à la *Jaws* for fear of it hurting local tourism.

However, if towns have learned anything from places like Roswell, New Mexico, or Point Pleasant, West Virginia, they should know that such stories tend to have the exact opposite effect on tourism.

Sources:

Coffey, Ron. *Kentucky Cryptids: "Monsters" of the Bluegrass State*. Fairy Ring Press, 2018.

Swancer, Brent. "The Bizarre Beast of the Land Between the Lakes." Mysterious Universe. (August 4, 2017) https://mysteriousuniverse.org/2017/08/the-bizarre-beast-of-the-land-between-the-lakes/

SKINWALKERS, WEREWOLVES, AND HELLHOUNDS OF NORTH AMERICA

SIDE STORY: WEREWOLF OR WILDMAN?

The following story was published in the *Hutchinson Daily News* out of Kansas on October 20, 1886, but the story itself takes place in Holmes County, Ohio. Though some view this as a possible Sasquatch or Wild Man story, I wonder if it might be a werewolf sighting?

A party of hunters, who have just returned from a hunt in the hills of Holmes County, say they encountered a curious creature on their trip. According to their description a wild man or some other strange being is at large in Holmes County. The party who report seeing this strange creature claim that he or it looked like a man, but acted like a wild beast. The creature was encountered near a brushy thicket and willow copse near what is known as Big Spring, where General Buell rested on his march through Ohio, at a point a short distance south of the Wayne County line in Holmes County. The hunters were beating the brush for pheasants when the attention of one of the party was attracted to an object that suddenly darted across an opening in the brush. Later on the object was again seen along the edge of the brush. By this time the hunters had reached open ground and were surprised to see what they describe as a man, entirely nude, but covered with what appeared to them to be matted hair. When seen he was some distance away, but on discovering the hunters started toward them on a run, and gave forth queer guttural sounds.

On seeing the strange being moving toward them the party of hunters, which included four persons all armed with shotguns, broke and ran. The strange creature pursued them for a short distance until the party had reached a public highway, when he turned back and was seen to enter Killbuck Creek, which he swam, and then disappeared in the brush again. On approaching the water he dropped on all fours and plunged like a dog, swimming like a canine. The hunters did not have the nerve to return, but got away from the place as soon as possible. They are emphatic in their assertion that they encountered a wild man, and describe him as above.

CHAPTER 4
WOLFMAN OF VERSAILLES

What follows is most likely just a tall tale with little to back it up, but it is interesting nonetheless. During the summer of 1863, the area of Versailles, Indiana, was attacked by a group of Confederate cavalrymen known as Morgan's Raiders.[9] The attacks lasted for over a month, and though they caused alarm in the North for a time, ultimately, they were considered a failure. (The goal of the raids was to draw Union soldiers back home to weaken their forces in the South).

Among the raiders was a soldier named Silas Shimmerhorn, who deserted while Morgan's Raiders were in Indiana—the reason being that

---

[9] Actually, it wasn't just Indiana, but parts of Ohio as well.

Shimmerhorn was himself born in Indiana and wished to return to his home state rather than go on aiding the Confederates. The problem now was that Silas was *persona non grata* among the Union and the Confederates alike. As such, he escaped to the wild and took refuge in a cave, today known as Bat Cave.

OLD ILLUSTRATION OF MORGAN'S RAIDERS.

For a time, Silas subsisted on killing game with his rifle, and when he ran out of bullets, he fashioned a bow and arrow to hunt with. Over time, Silas became quite unkempt in his appearance, having let his hair and beard grow without ever trimming either. According to legend, Silas began sharing his kills with a local wolf pack, who so appreciated his offerings that they accepted him as one of their own. Eventually, Silas let himself become one of the pack, going with them to raid farms in the night to make off with chickens and kill cattle. Farmers noticed the hairy, unkempt man

As for another odd detail to this werewolf-related case, Versailles, Indiana, is named for Versailles, France. No surprise there, but it's interesting to note that the legendary werewolf-like creature known as the Beast of Gévaudan, which terrorized 18th century France, was stuffed and sent to Versailles after it was finally killed.

wearing nothing but grey trousers running with the wolves, and the legend of "the Wolf Man of Versailles" was born.

Eventually, people got fed up with the raids, and hunters tracked the wolves back to their abode at Bat Cave but were soon driven away due to the fearsome beasts. Hunters also occasionally laid traps for Silas, who some whispered had lost the ability to speak and had become a true animal himself. Others were more compassionate and wished to help Silas rejoin society, as prejudices from the war days were beginning to simmer down.

As the years carried on, Silas's mental state continued to degrade, and he was now spotted completely nude as he ran with the wolf pack.

One year, the raids from Silas and his wolf pack became too much, and hunters vowed to hunt down the wolves once and for all. Over time, kill by kill, the hunters thinned the wolf pack. Eventually, so few wolves remained that the hunters were finally able to access Bat Cave. They never did find Silas, but they did find his bedding and a rifle with his initials engraved on it.

Long after he should have been dead, people still sighted Silas running with the wolves. In fact, even today some claim to see a spectral wolf pack with a naked wild man among their numbers roaming the wilds of Versailles...

CHAPTER 5
MYSTERY OF THE DOG EATER

The beast about to be described in this chapter is less a werewolf and more a canine cryptid, albeit one with strange attributes. Some might even say supernatural...

For several years denizens in the vicinity of Danville, Kentucky were terrorized by a creature that they dubbed the "dog eater." The reign of terror began in 1885 and continued sporadically into the 1890s. Like so many monsters before it, the "dog eater" was given a myriad of different characteristics and traits. A consistent behavior the beast exhibited was tearing off the heads of animals and leaving the bodies behind. An odd, one-off trait it once exhibited was draining the blood of its prey and not eating the body like a vampire.

In terms of description, it was a quadrupedal mammal. Its size varied, as was to be expected, and witnesses could never seem to make up their mind as to whether it was a panther, a huge dog, or even a bear.

The first article that I found on the beast was published in the April 7, 1885 edition of the *Hopkinsville Semi Weekly South Kentuckian* on the front page. As you'll see within the first few sentences, witnesses were certainly not in agreement as to what they were seeing. Were different animal sightings all attributed to the Dog Eater, or could it perhaps have been a shapeshifter?

The "Dog Eater."

The sensation of the day is the so-called Dog Eater. That an animal of some sort has been roaming about the country, and that it has killed a number of dogs, is sufficiently established. As to the description of the animal accounts differ very widely. Some say it looks like a lion, others think it more like a bengal tiger, another that it is like an alligator. The preponderance of the evidence, however, seems to be to the effect that it is black, and differing from a large Newfoundland dog mostly by its great length. It first attracted attention in the western part of Boyle, migrated to the eastern part of Marion, went back to Boyle, and was heard from last week in Washington County. The mystery surrounding the nature and movements of the beast soon fired the popular imagination, and upon the few facts known about it here has sprung up a vast and fantastic mythology.

Only three days later, the *Stanford Semi Weekly Interior Journal* ran another story about how a local man, Henry Owens, had been stalked by the beast as he walked to town. The same paper reported on June 17, 1887, that a strange animal had been seen on the farm of Roy Arnold. The man's son saw the beast and described it as being yellow in color, three feet long, and having a bushy tail. Despite only being three feet long, he claimed that its teeth were 12 inches!

Our next mention of the beast comes from this article from the *Columbus Enquirer* on November 23, 1888:

> The greatest sensation of Jasper county now is created by what is called a dog eater. It goes at night to different houses, and wherever it finds a small dog, or one it can easily conquer, it kills it and eats its head off. No one knows what the thing is, and there is considerable excitement over it.

Though it was supposedly seen off and on for the next several years, I can find no other account of it until the *Cincinnati Commercial Gazette* published the following on July 20, 1891, on page two. This account is especially of interest because it is in this one that the beast exhibited traits of a vampire:

A DOG DESTROYER.

COWBOYS & DOGMEN

A Mysterious Monster That Is Rapidly Reducing the Canine Population of Casey County, Ky.

Danville, Ky., July 19.—[Special.]—The peaceful residents in the vicinity of the village of Dunnville, in Casey County, are just now very much exercised and nonplussed by the appearance of a strange and destructive animal in their neighborhood, and which, for the want of a better appellation, they term "the dog-eater." Some three years ago the people of the west end of this county were the victims of the depredations of a similar animal, and the name of "the dog-eater" was given it because it preyed upon the canine tribe exclusively, and seemingly having an appetite for no other game. He suddenly disappeared from that section, however, much to the relief of the inhabitants and the local newspapers, and it was hoped that his absence would be permanent. But the animal is now creating the furore in Casey County, which is comparatively only a short distance from the scene of the former trouble, must be the original "dog-eater." The first indication of his return was last Tuesday night, or Wednesday morning rather, when Mr. G. R. Williams, who owns a large pack of fox hounds, went out to where the dogs had been chained the night before and found every one of them stark dead. There was very little evidence of a struggle, and for quite a while Mr. Williams could form no idea of the manner in which his dogs met their death.

SKINWALKERS, WEREWOLVES, AND HELLHOUNDS OF NORTH AMERICA

After a second and more careful examination he found that each dog had a small wound in the throat, and he soon saw that whatever did the work overpowered the poor brutes with very little difficulty, and then perforating their throats, sucked their life blood. The report of the affair soon spread abroad, and large numbers of the neighbors came in during the day to view the work of destruction, a great many of them thought it the work of a panther, or "painter," as the backwoodsmen term those ferocious beasts, but this could not be, as the panther feeds upon the entire carcass. Hunting parties were formed, as had been two years before in the Perryville neighborhood, but with the same futile results. Not being able to ascertain its hiding place, the country folks decided to endeavor to lure the mysterious visitor to the scene of Tuesday night slaughter, and they accordingly secured a worthless cur and tied it in a place convenient for watching the proceedings. A party of the farmers, heavily armed, hid in ambush Thursday night and patiently awaited the appearance of "the dog-eater." Through the long hours of the night they watched. Twelve, one and two o'clock came, and no dog-eater broke the silence. Just as the sentries were about to give up, however, a whine was heard, and they looked in the direction of the imprisoned cur, and the sight that met their gaze almost froze the blood in their veins.

The moon was shining brightly, and over the crouching form of the decoy dog they saw an immense white animal, unlike any other they had ever seen. They say it was built upon the greyhound pattern, but larger in every way, being four feet high and about six feet from the end of its tail to the tip of its nose or snout. So interested and frightened were they that not a gun was fired, and after the strange beast had finished its meal it calmly galloped away. The men went to the dead dog and found that it had been wounded in the same way as the hounds killed two nights before.

This is undoubtedly the same animal seen in the west end of this county two years ago. It was then seen by various parties, and the description they gave tallies with the one given above. One gentleman, who saw it attack a dog, says when the dog saw the "dog-eater" it was overcome with terror and seemed to be unable to move or to defend itself, and fell an easy victim to the enemy. The tracks left by the animal are similar to those made by a bird, though of course magnified many times, and showing that it has powerful talons.

Though the fact that the animal drank blood might liken it to a Chupacabra, back then, the Chupacabra was not a part of American folklore, nor did the animal sighted greatly match the bloodsucker's description. That they compare the tracks to those made by a bird is truly bizarre. Before moving on, it should be noted that this was the only instance where the "dog eater" drank blood. (Considering the bird-like footprints and the blood-drinking, perhaps this was a shapeshifting vampire along the lines of Mexico's Tlahuelpuchi, which often transformed into different types of birds and occasionally canines?)

By 1892, the Dog Eater had traveled south to Tennessee. The *Brownsville Daily Herald* out of Texas reported on the beast's depredations there in its December 28, 1892 edition. The story reported how the area was in a furor over the beast, which had a nasty habit of decapitating dogs. Locals described it as looking like a calf with fetters (chains) attached to its neck. This detail, too, is quite interesting, as it aligns with hellhound sightings in Mexico. Called Cadejos (covered in a later chapter), these unique hellhounds sometimes had hooves in place of regular paws and chains draped about their necks. Furthermore, the article claimed that the beast had fiery eyes, another attribute of a Cadejo (or any hellhound for that matter). Cadejo or not, like so many articles of the era, it concluded by supposing that it was an escaped circus animal, in this case, a panther.

The following article appeared in the *Evening Times* out of Monroe, Wisconsin, on October 28, 1893, and it, too, gave it fiery eyes:

A MONSTROUS BRUTE

Nothing Like It Known To The Most Eminent Zoologists

COWBOYS & DOGMEN

It Has a Broad Body, Flat Head, Big Fiery Eyes, Woolly Hide, Bushy Tail, Powerful Limbs and Bleeding Mouth.

The "dog eater," panther, or whatever it is that has created consternation time and again throughout the section among the country folks, has again made its appearance, after an interval of something like a year, says a Danville (Ky.) dispatch to the Cincinnati Enquirer. The existence of the strange animal has been scoffed at by the skeptics, but persons of undoubted veracity who claim to have seen the monster during its midnight prowling say they are willing to make oath to the statements concerning it.

About five years ago it made its appearance in this country and several parties were organized in the vicinity of Perryville to hunt the strange beast down and exterminate it, but none were successful in their mission. From the fact that it seldom, if ever, attacked anything save dogs, the people gave it the name of the "dog eater," and by this it has been known for about seven years. Persons versed in natural history say they can recall nothing like it, and seem to think, from the descriptions given by those who have caught glimpses of the animal, that it is a cross between a panther and a mastiff, though the descriptions vary so at times that such a conclusion cannot be relied upon.

Its last appearance was in Mercer County, a short distance from the city. James O'Connor and the colored driver of R.E. Coleman's bus were returning from Burgin with several passengers aboard, and had just passed the old Walden farm and were coming downhill at a moderately rapid gate, when suddenly the team stopped, reared, snorted and plunged about, almost upsetting the bus and badly frightening the passengers, acting just as horses have been seen to do when scared by some strange beast.

In a moment the occupants of the vehicle were startled and almost paralyzed at seeing an animal of enormous size and ferocious looks spring out of the woodland into the road, glare at the conveyance a moment and then leisurely leave the scene without molesting anything. The animal was distinctly seen by Mr. O'Connor and the driver, who were sitting upon the front seat. They describe it as being of a dark color, with a broad, flat like body and head, large, fiery eyes, woolly hide, powerful limbs, bushy tail and a monstrous head and mouth. There can be no doubt of Mr. O'Connor having seen this animal, as he would not concoct such a strange story, and his testimony about the appearance of the beast is corroborated by others who have seen it.

The question asked many by is: what is this monster that comes and goes, and still molests nothing except the worthless curs of the country, except now and then destroying a fancy setter? It is no stranger in Mercer County. Several years back there was a current report that some strange animal had taken up its abode in Boone's cave, and the people there about, especially the colored portion, were very much alarmed, and afraid to venture out after night. A few determined ones, however, explored the cave, but failed to find the monster, though they discovered strange looking tracks in the moist earth on the floor of the cave.

...

THAT MOST WONDERFUL ANIMAL.

ILLUSTRATION BY MR. FOX.

A year or so after this several parties in the vicinity of Burgin claim to have seen this nocturnal visitor, and numerous dead dogs, some almost completely devoured and others scarcely touched, attested to the existence of some fell destroyer. After a career of about three months in that vicinity the monster was next heard of in Casey county, where it appeared one night and destroyed twelve fine hound dogs belonging to a hunter living near Dunnville. The owner of these dogs concluded he would kill the pestiferous animal, and so he tied a dog to a stake and awaited its return on another night. While watching for the beast he fell asleep, and toward midnight he was awakened by the yelp of the dog he had tied, he jumped to his feet, gun in hand, just in time to see the game he was after disappearing over the hill, the dog's head having been bitten off. This was the last time the strange animal was seen in Casey county.

...

Mr. Woodford G. Portwood, of this city, says he plainly saw the dog-eater one night while he was with a fishing party on Dick's river. Mr. Portwood was some distance from camp, unaccompanied, save by his valuable pointer dog Jeff, that follows him wherever he goes. He was attending to a number of poles which he had set for catfish, and Jeff had wandered up the river some distance, when Mr. Portwood was attracted by a commotion in the bushes, accompanied by loud grunts and the howling of his dog Jeff. Directly the dog came rapidly running toward him, followed by a ferocious looking beast, which stopped as soon as it had seen the owner of the dog, looked at Mr. Portwood a moment, its eyes like two burning balls of fire, turned and went back into the bushes. The dog was trembling like a leaf, and has never been induced to go back to that particular spot of the river since. Colonel Thorp Shaw, who was in the camp that night, corroborates Mr. Portwood's story to the extent that he also heard the loud howling of the dog and that Portwood immediately left the catfish poles to take care of themselves until morning.

Two other gentlemen, Mr. Phil Marks and Edward H. Fox, the artist, claimed to have seen this remarkable beast one night as they were returning from a coon hunting expedition. They were riding leisurely along the pike, engaged in conversation, their fine pack of hounds following behind, wary and worn out after the chase, when suddenly Mark's horse reared up and had it not been for Mr. Marx's expert horsemanship he would have been thrown backward against the ground. Mr. Fox, who preserved his presence of mind, soon saw the cause of the trouble. The dog eater had stepped out into the road ahead of the party and began drinking out of a small stream, and right here this animal's strange influence over dogs was illustrated. The hounds following along seemed to become paralyzed with fright. They huddled together trembling with fear and whining piteously. Mr. Fox drew his revolver and shot at the dog eater, which jumped over the fence and disappeared. The artist is confident that he hit the monster, but thinks that the thick coating of hair on it was too much for the small bullet used. After the animal had got out of the way the hounds struck for home at a 2:40 gait. Mr. Marx can be found at his place of business in the city at any time, and will cheerfully detail the story of his experience with the now noted animal. Mr. Fox, at the request of the reporter, made a rough sketch of the dog eater as it appeared to him.

Considering that Fox was an artist, I suppose we should consider his sketch (reprinted on page 48) to be an accurate representation of the creature. For if it were a normal mountain lion or panther, would he not draw it as such? Fox's animal doesn't look like any cat I've ever seen, and Fox also gave it webbed feet. This would seem to corroborate the statements in the 1891 article about the beast's footprints: "The tracks left by the animal are similar to those made by a bird, though of course magnified many times, and showing that it has powerful talons." Lastly, the face is disturbingly human-looking. Could it have been a shapeshifter?

Whatever it was, it's possible that the "dog eater" was killed in 1893. However, its description is somewhat more mundane and certainly doesn't seem to match Mr. Fox's drawing. The story was reported in the *Cincinnati Commercial Gazette* on November 26, 1893, on page ten:

THE DOG EATER.
Peculiar, Animal the Terror of Farmers, Killed In Kentucky.

Harrodsburg, Ky., November 25.—(Special.)— For several years a strange animal has infested this locality. Taking Harrodsburg as a center, this peculiar quadruped has been seen within a radius of ten miles at different times and places.

Between High Bridge and Burgen, two years since, the natives were afraid to venture out of doors after dark lest they would encounter the dog-eater, as he was familiarly called. He was said to be a regular "Jack the Ripper" on dogs especially, killing every dog that chanced to come in his way. No dog could be made to encounter this ferocious animal. Many incredulous stories were circulated in regard to the different times the dog-eater was seen, and the number of canines he had destroyed.

A few months ago a vehicle loaded with passengers was being drawn to Harrodsburg when the docile team took fright at a strange, peculiar arrival that crossed the road, and a catastrophy narrowly averted. All parties concerned agreed that this was a visitation of the veritable dog-eater.

Yesterday there was a report current on the street that the dog-eater had been killed and that his skin was to be seen at a saloon. Hundreds went to see it. There it was, in the back room, on exhibition, the hide of the notorious dog-eater. It was about eight feet long from end of nose to tip of tail and from two to four feet in height. This dog-eater was shot the day before in the vicinity of Perryville, ten miles from this place. He had massacred several dogs and was making said havoc in a flock of sheep when a farmer named Taylor shot him with a load of buck-shot.

This animal was no doubt a cross between a she wolf and a Newfoundland dog. Still many claim it is of a species purely its own, and is the dog-eater, and nothing else.

There is a range of low, rocky hills that traverse this State, called "The Knobs," that are distant not more than three or four miles from Perryvllle, where this strange creature was killed. Some years since a wolf was killed in this locality; and as it was a male, the female was supposed to have been left to roam the hills by herself. This mongrel that had been killed was a terror to children and colored people of all ages.

This strange animal had been frequently seen in the vicinity of Perryville, and is said to have galloped instead of being able to run like a dog.[10]

THE BEAST OF GÉVAUDAN.

Whether it was a werewolf, a hellhound, or some form of cryptid canine akin to the Beast of Gévaudan, the Dog Eater was never seen again in Kentucky.

---

[10] This galloping motion was also described in the 1891 article.

PORTRAIT OF YEIBICHAI DANCER BY
EDWARD S. CURTIS c.1904 OFTEN
MISLABELED AS A SKINWALKER.

CHAPTER 6
PLAGUE OF THE SKINWALKERS

Between August of 1864 to the end of 1866 occurred the tragic "Long Walk" or "Trail of Tears." During that time, the Navajo people made an arduous trek from Arizona and Western New Mexico to the Bosque Redondo Indian Reservation in Fort Sumner, New Mexico.[11] During the course of those two years, thousands of Navajos in over fifty separate groups were forced to make the traumatic journey across the desert to Bosque Redondo. To make matters worse, they would have to share Bosque Redondo with their old enemies, the Mescalero Apache. By 1868 the endeavor was officially acknowledged as a failure, and all the Navajo were allowed to return home to

---

[11] If the place name of Fort Sumner rings a bell, that's because that's where outlaw Billy the Kid was killed in 1881.

the place they called Dinehtah, or Navajoland. But, the horrors and ramifications of the Long Walk weren't over yet, because, like many other historical events, the aftermath of the Long Walk has a hidden history veiled in the supernatural.

A U.S. CAVALRYMAN STANDS WATCH DURING THE LONG WALK.

When the Navajo returned to their homeland in 1868, they did so without adequate provisions for the journey. As such, when they settled back to what they thought would be their old lives in Dinehtah, they fell upon hard times. There was great sickness among the people and their livestock alike. Arousing suspicions, probably based upon jealousy part of the time, was the fact that some families prospered with their livestock and farms while others suffered badly. Some blamed this sickness, along with other hardships, on witchcraft. Over the next decade, the whispers of witchcraft would grow louder until they finally reached a fever pitch in the summer of 1878.

SKINWALKERS, WEREWOLVES, AND HELLHOUNDS OF NORTH AMERICA

According to the Navajo, there were four types of witchcraft that could be perpetrated, identified as witchery, sorcery, wizardry, and frenzy witchcraft. It was the middle two categories, sorcery and witchery, that made up the bulk of the allegations in the Navajo Witch Purge of 1878. Of the four categories, the middle two made up the bulk of allegations during 1878. Sorcery in the Navajo context referred to the burial of property of victims or pieces of the victims themselves, and witchery in this sense meant people being hit or injected with foreign projectiles. For instance, the bone dart is the most dreaded weapon of many Native American cultures, and it was often fired by a skinwalker.

The notorious skinwalkers are most common to the Navajo, though a few other Native American tribes have variations of them, and all could change into different animals. Or, in other words, they were Native American werewolves. Only they didn't just transform into wolves, they could also become foxes, coyotes, and other animals common to the Southwest including types of birds.

Today, "skinwalker" is a term that the layman knows the creatures by, but the Navajo themselves call them "yee naaldlooshii" or, "with it, he goes on all fours." Whereas tribal medicine men used their knowledge to heal the sick, the skinwalkers used theirs to harm and commit evil deeds. Their most powerful "medicine" was corpse powder, the dried-up, crushed bone powder of the dead. Also common were the aforementioned bone darts, fired at their victims to cause sickness.

As to how one became a skinwalker, the finer points are still shrouded in mystery for the most part, but the final phase of the initiation occurred after one had killed either a sibling or a close relative. To induce the transformation from man to beast, the skinwalker must wear the pelt of the animal they wish to transform into. Sometimes they might also wear the skull of the animal atop their heads, as it was thought this increased their power. They would pick their animal based upon the task at hand. If they wanted speed, they might choose a fleet four-footed animal like a wolf, or even a mountain lion of some sort.[12] If they wanted brute strength, they might choose a bear, for instance. For this reason, one won't see a regular Navajo wearing the pelt of a predatory animal, as the skinwalkers made it taboo.

The skinwalker's powers didn't stop at shapeshifting; they were also able to possess people. Perhaps possession isn't the right word, as it wasn't implied that their spirit entered their victim's body so much as they could gain control over a person after locking eyes with them for too long.

And how might one spot a skinwalker? Well, in human form, they are said to have animal-like eyes, while in animal form, their eyes appear more human-like and will also glow red when a bright light is shown upon them.

---

[12] *Cowboys & Saurians South of the Border* has a tale of a Skinwalker that transformed into the cryptid big cat the Onza.

SKINWALKERS, WEREWOLVES, AND HELLHOUNDS OF NORTH AMERICA

ANOTHER YEIBICHAI DANCER BY EDWARD S. CURTIS.

Though witchcraft had always been a despised but acknowledged part of the Navajo existence, what kicked off what would later be known as the Navajo Witch Purge was the chilling discovery of a "cursed item" in the first half of 1878. Apparently, a Navajo had found the "cursed item" buried in the Arizona desert near Ganado Lake, only being a good Navajo, this person couldn't touch the cursed item. As such, a trusted trader named Charles Hubbell was recruited to do so. Charles was the less well-known brother of Juan "Don" Lorenzo Hubble, who along with his brother, was born in San Miguel County, New Mexico. Together the two established a franchise of trading posts across the Southwest.

JUAN LORENZO HUBBELL.

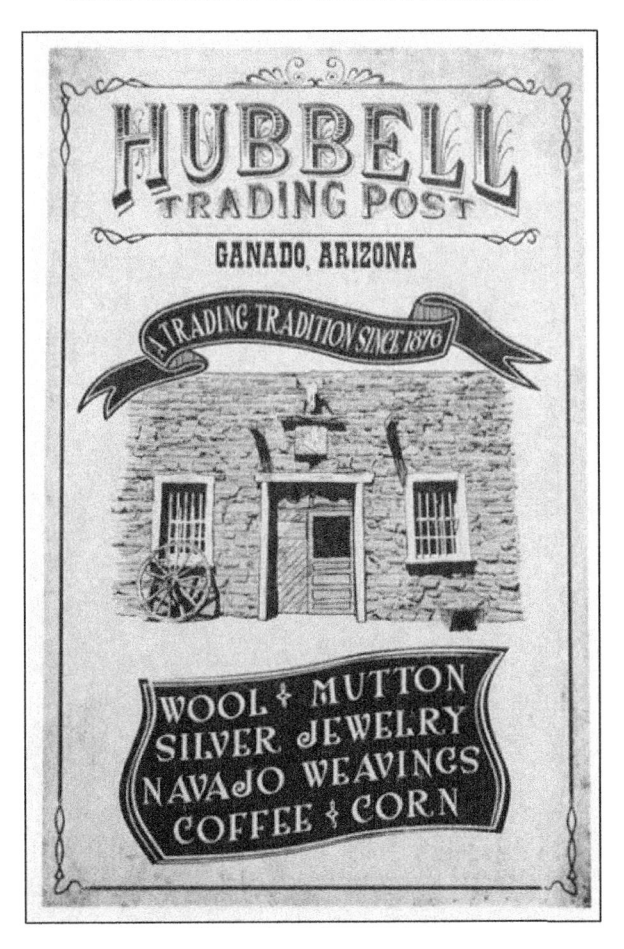

SKINWALKERS, WEREWOLVES, AND HELLHOUNDS OF NORTH AMERICA

HUBBELL TRADING POST
GANADO, ARIZONA
A TRADING TRADITION SINCE 1876

WOOL & MUTTON
SILVER JEWELRY
NAVAJO WEAVINGS
COFFEE & CORN

Eventually, the brothers developed quite a rapport with the Navajo and began trading with them. One of the ways in which the Hubbells benefited the Navajo (and themselves) was in helping them to determine which patterns on their blankets were the most popular among consumers so that they would know what to produce more of.

Of Hubbell, it was said that "Sentiment about him varied. Euro-Americans viewed him as the dean of Indian traders in the Southwest. Some Navajo customers said it was good to have trader Hubbell as a friend, while others said Navajos did everything around his trading ranch for low wages."[13]

---

[13] Blue, *Indian Trader: The Life and Times of J. L. Hubbell*, p.9.

SKINWALKERS, WEREWOLVES, AND HELLHOUNDS OF NORTH AMERICA

As stated before, the Navajos requested that Charles Hubbell go and remove the cursed item found near Ganado Lake. Hubbell agreed and made a chilling discovery. Though accounts differ on what he found, the most interesting alleges that within a shallow grave, Hubbell found a dead body with the stomach split open. Within the stomach, he found either a curse scrawled across a random piece of paper or the actual 1868 treaty between the Navajo and the U.S. government that had released them from Bosque Grande.

A grandson of a tribal member named Hash keh yilnaya years later recollected to researcher Martha Blue that "the collection that these witches gathered was found wrapped in paper and this paper was I think the Treaty of 1868...buried in the belly of a dead person in a grave...."[11]

The unearthing of this cursed item set about a series of events comparable to the Salem Witch Trials of the late 1600s, only much less publicized, and which resulted in an estimated 40 people being executed as skinwalkers or witches. While some of the executed persons may well have been actual skinwalkers, it is believed that plenty of others were just the victims of malicious false allegations motivated by jealousy and petty feuds.

The first skinwalker to die was executed right in front of Hubbell's Trading Post, possibly in the doorway itself. Years later, an elderly tribesman named Yazzie T'iis Yazh related the following to researcher Martha Blue:

> Hastiin Jieh Kaal/Digoli was first killed in the doorway of Hubbell's first trading post near the lake after he told about his companion killing young people. After that the trading post was relocated to the present site because Navajos were afraid of the trading post where Hastiin Jieh Kaal/Digoli was slain and considered the building haunted.

---

[14] Ibid, p.9.

SKINWALKERS, WEREWOLVES, AND HELLHOUNDS OF NORTH AMERICA

YEIBICHAI DANCERS PHOTOGRAPHED BY EDWARD S. CURTIS.

Whoever killed the skinwalker in front of Hubbell's lucrative trading post made a poor decision in location, as the Navajo belief system warns that the dead spirit of a violent killing will linger at the kill spot. As such, Hubbell moved his post to a location nearer Ganado Lake.[15] Yazh said,

> ....in the doorway there was blood all over, so the people living around there told [Hubbell] that he shouldn't live in a place where someone dies.[16]

---

[15] This wasn't likely due to Hubbell sharing that belief so much as he knew the Navajo held that belief and would no longer frequent his post.
[16] Blue, *Indian Trader: The Life and Times of J. L. Hubbell*, pp.8-9.

Soon after, the Navajo went after the Hastiin Jieh Kaal's companion that he had accused of killing young people. Yazh related to Blue that,

[H]is companion was Hastiin Biwosi and was in the vicinity performing a ceremony so some Navajos went there to kill Hastiin Biwosi.[17]

According to some accounts, as many as 50 people went out in search of Biwosi. A grandson of one of the posse, Hash keh yilnaya, said that "people gathered... from Ganado, and some from Greasewood, and others from Klagetoh... they prepared themselves... armed themselves with guns, arrows, clubs... there were many people riding horses... fifty... or hundred.[18]

Where exactly the posse found Biwosi has never been specified, but find him they did in some kind of residence. They stated their business to the inhabitants of the structure, all of whom left, and the party then drug Biwosi outside. There, a respected leader of the tribe, Totsohnii Hastiin, officially pronounced Biwosi as a witch and all but one were set to kill him, that being Ganado Mucho, who cried, "[H]e's my relative... my older brother!"[19]

In some accounts, it was also stated that Mucho made the case that as dangerous as a skinwalker was in life, its ghost could be even more deadly.

---

[17] Ibid, p.9.
[18] Ibid, pp.9-10.
[19] Ibid, p.11.

However, Hash keh yilnaya argued that Biwosi had "cut off [his] chance for a good life. . ."[20] Totsohnii Hastiin then gave the go-ahead to kill Biwosi, and the group shot him and then stoned him to death.[21]

Following Biwosi's death, tensions continued to escalate throughout Dinehtah. Charles Hubbell and his employees feared that since their post had been the sight of the first killing that they may be implicated in it somehow. By late spring, Hubbell was concerned enough with the "Witch Purge" to write a letter to "W.B. Leonard, Fort Defiance, Arizona Territory, Yavapai County" on May 31, 1878. In the letter, he requested that he be sent rifles and ammunition because he was expecting a "big row" among the Navajo. Specifically, he felt that a large band of them may arrive from Canyon de Chelly, Arizona, to attack most of the Anglo settlers, and in particular, he feared for his store being destroyed.

In another letter written on the same day, Hubbell revealed he had received intel from an informant he identified only as Ganio, that certain Indians were arming themselves and had intent to harm him specifically. As such, he requested that soldiers from Fort Defiance come and protect him, his family, and their post.[22]

---

[20] Ibid.
[21] Reportedly, even Mucho participated in the killing despite his earlier protests. However, he later feared that due to his "serious transgression, the killing of a relative" that he would suffer retaliation of some sort.
[22] It is unknown if these letters was written before or after the killing of Hastiin Biwosi.

FORT WINGATE, NEW MEXICO.

Sometime later, Manuelito—another Navajo tribal leader—arrived at Fort Wingate with a letter he had written to J. L. Hubbell—stating that "the Navajos had tied up six medicine men accused of witchcraft" and that he was convinced many Navajos would start murdering each other without military intervention. As to why Manuelito himself wasn't caught up in the witch hunt, it was because his own cousin had been executed earlier that summer.

Eventually, the military intervened as requested. Ten accused witches were then brought before a military council presided over by Lieutenant D. D. Mitchell. Instead of having them executed as the Navajo would have done, he let them go and gave a stern speech condemning the wanton killing of the alleged witches. After this, the killings lessened in number, though a few still occurred in isolated areas from time to time. But, for the most part, the Navajo Witch Purge of 1878 was over.

Of course, today we brush off the 1878 witchcraft claims as pure unfounded superstition. And while most of them probably were false claims based upon petty feuds, how many more might have concerned true supernatural evil? After all, there are still many sightings of skinwalkers in Navajo country today...

Sources:

Allison, A. Lynn. "The Navajo Witch Purge Of 1878." *Arizona State University West Literary Magazine* (May 2001). www.west.asu.edu//paloverde-/Paloverde2ooi/Witch, him.

Blue, Martha. *Indian Trader: The Life and Times of J. L. Hubbell.* Kiva Publishing, Inc., 2000.

---------------------*The Witch Purge of 1878.* Navajo Community College Press, 1988.

ILLUSTRATION FROM *HOUND OF THE BASKERVILLES*, WHICH UTILIZED THE HELL HOUND LEGEND.

CHAPTER 7
HELL DOGS OF EL DORADO

In modern popular culture, relatively speaking at least, the idea of the demon dog or hellhound was probably best popularized in *The Omen* (1976). In that film, big black spectral dogs guard the antichrist in child form. Though this may have been the introduction of the hellhound for many, as you can imagine, the legend of the hellhound originated in Europe, and the most famous was that of Black Shuck.

Black Shuck made his debut during a strange thunderstorm in Suffolk on August 4, 1577. The hellish hound burst through the doors of a church, ran down the aisle, and killed a man and a boy. Where his paws had tread seemed to be burnt as if by fire.

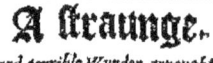

> **A straunge**
> and terrible Wunder wrought
> very late in the parish Church
> of Bongay, a Town of no great di-
> stance from the citie of Norwich, namely
> the fourth of this August, in ÿ yeere of
> our Lord 1577. in a great tempest of vio-
> lent raine, lightning, and thunder, the
> like whereof hath been sel-
> dome seene.
> With the appearance of an horrible sha-
> ped thing, sensibly perceived of the
> people then and there
> assembled.
> Drawen into a plain method ac-
> cording to the written coppye.
> by Abraham Fleming.

BLACK SHUCK

The Americas have their hellhounds too. The ones most distinctive to the Old West are those said to haunt Eldorado Canyon in Nevada. The name of the canyon is ironic for a number of reasons, chief among them that it was named El Dorado canyon before gold was ever discovered there by Europeans. The Spanish named the area during their initial exploration, even though all they found there were silver veins. In the 1850s, a group of prospectors did discover gold there, and by 1858, as more people made their way up the Colorado River, the secret of the gold was out, and miners flooded the area. As such, El Dorado became one of the wildest spots of the Wild West.

In the early 1860s, a decent number of the miners comprised of Civil War deserters. Eventually, 500 men had amassed in the area to mine for gold. As usual, men killed each other either over women or gold.[23] The locale had such a lawless reputation, where killing was a daily occurrence that lawmen reportedly avoided the area and some even called it Helldorado.

---

[23] North and South tensions also resulted in some killings as well.

**ELDORADO CANYON FROM THE
COLORADO RIVER, C. 1900-1925.
(UNLV SPECIAL COLLECTIONS)**

Kathy Weiser said it best on Legends of America when she wrote,

> Man per man and mile per mile, Eldorado Canyon has a wider range of historical events than anywhere in the Wild West. This rich history, coupled with the turbulent events taking place in Eldorado Canyon in the 19th century has led to numerous ghost stories of dead miners, Indians, and pioneers who once roamed the area.[24]

Among the most famous of Eldorado's spooks are easily the hellhounds. However, whereas most hellhounds are aligned in some way with the devil

---

[24] https://www.legendsofamerica.com/hell-dogs-of-eldorado-canyon/

and said to come from hell itself, hence the namesake, Eldorado's ghostly dogs have a unique origin all their own. Appropriately, they stem from the area's gold-boom heyday. In those days, prospectors kept vicious dogs chained up at their claim sites to protect them in the night, much like the junkyard dogs of today.

While some of these dogs may have been well-treated and cared for by their owners, according to legend, many others were not. When the miners began to leave the area in the first half of the 20th Century, many of the poor dogs were simply either shot or left staked to their chains to starve to death as they were no longer needed. The lucky ones were either taken home or released into the wild.

Today, spectral black dogs are the most commonly seen ghosts among Eldorado... supposedly. A user on the Shadowlands.net wrote of their experience in Eldorado seeing the legendary hellhounds. The author and his brother had heard of the legend and decided to explore the Eldorado region north of Hoover Dam. Their first few trips didn't yield any evidence of the dogs, spectral or otherwise. On their final visit, they found an eight-foot chain embedded into the rocks at the entrance to a mine shaft. The brothers entered the mine shaft and found the bones of a very large dog. But still, no spooks showed up. Either feeling confident that there were no ghosts, or perhaps hoping still to see one, the brothers made camp outside of the mine shaft. That night, they could hear the howls of what they assumed were coyotes when suddenly,

The atmosphere became thick and very uneasy. We now felt that we were being watched from a very close distance. What we thought was the night time breeze now sounded more like the panting or breathing of large dogs in close proximity. Then we heard the growling. Grating, low......and hatefull [sic]. The fall of paws on the desert sand now became apparent. They seemed to circle the campsite. We were surrounded.[25]

Next, the brothers' attention was drawn to a scratching noise coming from the entrance to the mine. They looked and could see the chain moving as though an invisible dog were attached to it. The chain began to tug away from the rock it was attached to while at the same time, scratch marks and blood began to appear on the rock. Finally, a hairy invisible something brushed against the author's leg. The brothers had gotten the ghostly encounter they had hoped for and promptly ran for their car. All the while, they could hear the ravenous panting and the rhythm of dogs feet pounding the dirt as they ran to the vehicle. The two men made it to their car and sped away. It was at this point that the ghostly dogs either materialized to become visible, or a live pack of dogs began following the car:

> On the road heading out of the canyon we were paced for a good two or three miles at least by

---

[25] http://theshadowlands.net/ghost/ghost137.htm

what seemed to be a pack of wild strays! We made it home and I will never forget the terror of being chased by this pack of spectral hounds...NEVER![26]

While an interesting story, it is actually only one of a few as it turns out. Truthfully, not as many people claim to see these "hellhounds" of Eldorado as you might think. Or, if they do, they mostly go unreported. Apart from the account published on the Shadowlands, only one other hellhound account can be dug up that relates to Eldorado. The ever-dependable Brent Swancer of Mysterious Universe found an account on the now-removed blog King Sasquatch Paranormal & Cryptozoology Blog.

The tale told of a group of friends out four-wheeling in Eldorado Canyon. One of the group saw what he took to be a coyote crouching in a "defensive stance" while his friends next to it could see no such thing (the implication being that he was seeing a ghost dog while they were not). Later that night, the shadow of a canine crept across the tent of one of the girls there, who screamed loudly at the sight of it. It is said that when she did, the animal disappeared, but the poster wasn't specific enough in their wording to clarify if he meant it ran away or faded away like a specter.

The same blog had one other account in which the witnesses were boating up the Colorado River in the vicinity of Eldorado Canyon. This account

---

[26] Ibid.

was a bit more interesting as it implied more of a flesh and blood cryptid rather than a ghost. The account was related by the father of one of the witnesses, who wrote,

> Around two in the morning my house phone rang off the hook with my son fanatically shouting that he had just seen a mutant dog with a piercing howl attempting to catch a duck. He forwarded the details as a four-foot mangy dog with terrifying overlapping teeth. He said the dog failed to catch ducks and ran off hungry when they shined a flashlight onto the shore.[27]

If not for its having been seen in the haunts of the hellhounds, one might well have lumped this sighting in with that of the mangy Chupacabra. Was it perhaps one of the living descendants of the prospectors' guard dogs set free into the wilds of the canyon, or did one of the spectral dogs manage to make a physical manifestation of itself?

Though sightings of these hellhounds are relatively few in number, due to their unique history, their legend has caught on quite well. They even attracted the attention of Jack Osbourne for his series *Haunted Highway* in 2102. In the episode where Jack and co. visit Eldorado Canyon, their thermal imaging cameras appeared to pick up a dog-like quadruped in the darkness, approaching one of the show's cohosts. In true *Blair Witch*

---

[27] https://mysteriousuniverse.org/2020/09/haunted-el-dorado-canyon-and-its-mysterious-hellhounds/

Project style, as the cohost runs through the desert, for a split-second, a dog-like beast is seen to jump across the screen and hit her on the shoulder and then disappear. Was it simple TV trickery or a real hellhound sighting? Considering that spooks and cryptids are loathe to show up for those actually hunting them, the former seems more likely.

Sources:

Swancer, Brent. "Haunted El Dorado Canyon and its Mysterious Hellhounds." Mysterious Universe (September 22, 2020) https://mysteriousuniverse.org/2020/09/haunted-el-dorado-canyon-and-its-mysterious-hellhounds/

Weiser, Kathy. "Hell Dogs of Eldorado Canyon." Legends of America. (updated February 2020) https://www.legendsofamerica.com/hell-dogs-of-eldorado-canyon/

SKINWALKERS, WEREWOLVES, AND HELLHOUNDS OF NORTH AMERICA

ANOTHER HELLHOUND TALE

Though not as interesting as the Hell Dogs of Eldorado, Oglethorpe County, Georgia, also played host to a hellhound, as shown in this article printed in the *Atlanta Constitution* on May 27, 1889:

A Ghost in Goosepond

That strip of country lying between Colonel Mike Mattox's and Millstone has always been considered as haunted ground, and a few years ago the good people living thereabout were greatly disturbed over the appearance in the public road of a strange looking wild animal that suddenly sprang up before them, or, if riding, beneath the feet of the horses, or under the wheels of the vehicles, but on being struck at with a whip would vanish from sight. This singular visitor only appeared at night, and was seen by a number of responsible white men, including Mr. A. G. Power, well known to our people, and we think also by Mr. Dock Mattox. It made periodical [sic] appearances for several months, when no more was heard of it.

"But recently this varmint, or whatever it is, has again began [sic] its pilgrimages, and has been seen several times recently, but this time only by American citizens of African descent. A few nights since . . . Perry Mattox, while near Mr. Mike Mattox's, suddenly noticed just in front of the wagon he was driving a strange little red colored quadruped, about the size of a dog, or perhaps somewhat larger. The mules noticed the thing as soon as the driver, and became terribly excited and frightened. They began to run away, but Perry managed to keep them in the road. When they slackened their gait the thing in front would also hold up, so as to keep a certain distance ahead. When it reached a point on the road where there is an old grave yard, the apparition seemed to glide among the tombs and then vanish from sight. Perry was badly frightened and firmly believes that he has seen a spirit.

"Several other Negroes report having recently seen this thing, and they say that whoever strikes at it shall instantly drop dead. It seems only to pursue solitary travelers, and makes its appearance about midnight. Sometime since it rushed between the legs of a Negro, and he says he could not feel it touch him. The thing then vanished from sight, to reappear in an instant about ten feet in advance of him, to again vanish in a grave yard. In fact, this little four-footed visitor seems to have its home among the numerous old burial grounds that dot the neighborhood."

CHAPTER 8
WATROUS WEREWOLF

In Northern New Mexico is a small community called Watrous. In the time before Anglo-settlement, the Watrous area was a crossroads, or junction, where many different Native American tribes met to trade, including the Comanche, Kiowa, Apache, Ute, and the Puebloans. What eventually came to be known as Watrous sprang from the Santa Fe Trail in the mid-1800s. Initially, it was called La Junta. Upon the arrival of Mora County farmer and trader Samuel B. Watrous, the area began to grow due to him building a large trading post. As you can guess, eventually La Junta came to be known as Watrous. Today the area is sparsely populated with a population of only 135, though it does have the distinction of being a National Historic Landmark District.[28]

WATROUS, NEW MEXICO.

According to Jack Kutz's landmark book, *Mysteries and Miracles of New Mexico*, Watrous was once the home of several skinwalkers. Unfortunately, Kutz doesn't say when these stories took place, but since both seem to be Spanish folktales, one might presume it was the early 1800s.[29] The first story goes that one night, past midnight, a young man "whose name no one remembers now" was riding his horse down a

---

[28] The settlement began its steady decline upon a 1910 fire that nearly burned down the entire town. The Great Depression of the 1930s sounded Watrous's true death knell and by 1950 the population had dwindled to around 250 people.
[29] Kutz included the story in his chapter entitled "Open Doors to the Spirit World". Our only indication is that the story took place pre-1885, as the story followed an entry on a murder from 1885 which Kutz implies this story pre-dates.

> The death of Samuel B. Watrous, though not related to the werewolf of this chapter, is interesting nonetheless as an aside. To this day Watrous's death remains unsolved. He was found near his home with two gunshot wounds to the head, which newspapers oddly supposed were self-inflicted. (How could one shoot one's self in the head twice?) Watrous's own son had committed suicide before that, and Watrous was naturally despondent over the fact and so the papers said he committed suicide himself with the very same gun. However, others think that not only was the elder Watrous murdered, but so was his son.

lonely road. The man had been visiting his cousin on a farm outside of town, and the two had stayed up late talking until they lost track of time, hence his late-night journey.

The lonely road was flanked on either side with plowed fields. His ride was uneventful until he came to a grove of cottonwood trees. Somewhere in the grove, he could hear a baby crying.[30] He dismounted his horse and looked around the area until he found a baby mysteriously hidden among the weeds. The man came to the abandoned baby's rescue, intending to take it back into town with him. When he approached his horse with the infant, the animal became upset. The man eventually calmed

---

[30] The baby crying warrants a relative aside in the lore of the skinwalker, as it is said that skinwalkers will imitate the sound of a baby crying to lure well-meaning people out to help what they assume is an abandoned infant. However, this story goes so far as to have the wicked being assume the form of a baby, which is a new one as far as I can tell.

his horse and climbed atop it with the baby in one arm.

As the horse trotted back to town, suddenly the baby spoke in the voice of a man. It told the rider that it didn't like riding this way and asked to be placed behind the man on the saddle. Terrified and not knowing what else to do, the young man moved the baby behind him onto the saddle. It clutched his waist with its tiny hands, which then supernaturally began to grow larger. At the same time the horse became panicked, and the rider did everything he could to bring it back under control. The rider was so distracted that he could hardly notice the hands getting bigger and the weight of his saddle growing heavier. As he felt the presence behind him growing larger, he heard something that sounded like the panting of an animal. He could even smell its noxious breath. At that point, he finally looked down at his waist. The tiny baby's hands had been replaced with hairy claws.

With dread, he turned his head to look behind him and saw a humanoid beast that he described as half-human and half-panther. When it shrieked, tellers of the tale embellished that the young man could hear "the screams of all the tormented souls in hell."[31]

The horse reared up in terror and succeeded in knocking off his master, but not the beast which was causing it so much panic. The young man watched from the ground in horror as the monster clung to his horse's back. Now he was able to get a

---

[31] Kutz, *Mysteries and Miracles of New Mexico*, p.86.

SKINWALKERS, WEREWOLVES, AND HELLHOUNDS OF NORTH AMERICA

better look at it. Like a panther, it also had a tail which he described as "whip-like" and also "long tangled hair." (Was he referring to the hair of its head or the whole body? Kutz doesn't specify.)

The young man watched helplessly as the horse and the monster ran off into the night. The man ran in the opposite direction, back to his cousin's home, where he told his terrifying tale. According to the legend, the cousin wouldn't have believed him if not for the man's badly torn jacket. The horse was never found and the monster disappeared forever.

Though this is clearly just a folktale, the Watrous area apparently had a penchant for supernatural animal stories. This one, too, comes courtesy of Kutz, who again doesn't specify the year. He only says that it was another tale to come from Watrous. Unlike the panther monster earlier, this one is more in line with typical werewolves and skinwalkers.

For a few nights once per month, the denizens of Watrous were terrorized by a black dog. It would slink into town on dark, moonless nights. There it would target and kill dogs belonging to locals. After a few nights of terror, it would disappear and not resurface until the following month. Eventually the townspeople set out to capture the sinister animal. The next time that the moon entered its darker cycle, the townsfolk hid in the shadows to wait for the dog.

Just as they hoped, it sauntered back into town. They sprang on it and beat it with ax handles and chunks of firewood.[32] (The fact that no one tried to shoot it seems to suggest this was the earlier village of La Junta rather than the town of Watrous.) The dog wasn't killed and ran off into the wild.

The next morning, it was business as usual in the town except for one thing: an old woman that lived on the edge of town had yet to be seen. Concerned for their elderly neighbor, several people went to check on her. Inside her home, they found her bruised and beaten nearly beyond recognition.

This folktale was likely an offshoot of one from the Sonora region of Mexico, where an elderly witch turned into a mountain lion every night to terrorize local children.[33] The witch/mountain lion folktale likely made its way up north via the Hispanic settlers of the region, which was probably also true of the other folktale. The only question I have is why did Watrous, of all places, inspire several folktales related to the skinwalker legend?

Sources:

Kutz, Jack. *Mysteries and Miracles of New Mexico.* Rhombus Books, 1988.

---

[32] That they beat the dog with an ax handle as opposed to the sharpened tip of the ax itself was rather telling. After all, if they had chopped it up with an ax and killed it, the story would lack the exciting ending of the old woman who was apparently unbeknownst to them a witch.

[33] You might be shocked to know that the usually reliable J. Frank Dobie infamously passed the Sonora skinwalker story off as real in one of his articles.

CHAPTER 9
BEFORE BRAY ROAD

Thanks to the Beast of Bray Road, Wisconsin, is probably the place in the U.S. today most associated with werewolves. Though it has been sighted for generations, the Wisconsin werewolf didn't become popular until the late 1980s when it was encountered along Bray Road in Walworth County. The sightings were then made famous by Linda Godfrey's reporting and her ensuing 2003 book *The Beast of Bray Road*. About 80 miles northwest of Bray Road took place the lesser-known account of the "Werewolf of Springfield Corners" in the mid-19th Century. The tale concerned an itinerant German dance instructor named Herr Gross.

COWBOYS & DOGMEN

VINTAGE WEREWOLF ENGRAVING.

SKINWALKERS, WEREWOLVES, AND HELLHOUNDS OF NORTH AMERICA

When strange deaths began plaguing the area of Springfield Corners, located at a crossroads northwest of Madison, locals turned a suspicious eye to Gross, who had come to the area sometime before the year 1848. Among the mysterious happenings was a housewife who saw a wolf-like monster outside. The shock made the woman fall and twist her ankle, and she claimed that the wolf laughed at her. Following this were the deaths of children, which, though due to an illness, were still blamed on witchcraft by a werewolf! A bit later, a farmer was killed on the way to Madison to buy a new horse. Though he was likely just killed by a robber to steal his gold coins, the death was still blamed on the werewolf. However, this story doesn't end with Gross being taken away and burned at the stake, as the days of the old Spanish Inquisition were long gone. Instead, locals simply whispered and spread rumors about Gross, who most likely was not a werewolf. As to the beast seen by the housewife, it would seem to be unrelated to the other incidents that plagued the area.

The next possible recorded werewolf sighting in Wisconsin occurred in 1867 in the vicinity of Oak Creek. I say possible werewolf sighting because some think this may have been a sasquatch or basic "wild man" as they were known in those days. I, however, take note of how the man-beast ran on all fours, and being in Wisconsin, one has to wonder if it was a werewolf. The story was published in the *Portsmouth Journal of Literature and Politics* on August 31, 1867:

The Milwaukee Sentinel tells a strange story about a man-beast, lately discovered in the vicinity of Oak Creek, Wisconsin. For some months the farmers in that neighborhood had been annoyed by the disappearance of their fowls. Doors were opened and roosts were robbed in the most summary and mysterious manner; and sometimes even lambs disappeared.

That these were not stolen by human hands was thought to be evident from the marks around of the fowls being eaten on the spot. One farmer determined to solve the mystery; and so, rifle in hand, he watched his premises.

At about 11 o'clock he discovered an animal of some kind approaching his hen house with stealthy step, sometimes going on all fours, and sometimes erect. He fired, and a piercing shriek, like that of a human being, showed that the creature had been hit. It nevertheless made off to the woods, where it was seen the subsequent day, having the face and hands of a human being and the hairy body of a beast. But though wounded it made its escape, and though subsequently seen again, had not been captured at last accounts.

About fifty miles to the north of Bray Road, in the vicinity of Deerfield, Wisconsin, a werewolf sighting occurred one afternoon in December of 1896.

It came courtesy of the December 20, 1896 *Milwaukee Sentinel* and was labeled as "A Ghost Story Told by Widow Olson." I found it in Jerome Clark's *Hidden Realms, Lost Civilizations, and Beings from Other Worlds,* partially reprinted on page 204.

The story goes that the widow Olson and her 14-year-old son were living along the shores of Stump Lake when they heard a knocking on their door one day. They opened it to find a mysterious boy asking for directions to the house of a farmer who lived across the lake. As the walk to the residence was about three miles, Mrs. Olson told her son to ferry the boy across the lake to save time.

SKINWALKERS, WEREWOLVES, AND HELLHOUNDS OF NORTH AMERICA

Out on the waters of the lake is when things got weird. According to the article, the passenger sat at the stern of the boat facing away from young Olson, who tried to engage the boy in conversation to no avail, as the strange boy sat in silence. Clark reprinted the following portion of the article, and I shall do the same:

> His strange behavior made Olson observe him more closely and the more closely and the more he looked at him, the more did he appear unlike a human. His attention was first attracted by the stranger's ears, which were abnormally large, reaching almost to the top of his head, where they came to nearly a point or sharp angle and were covered with a fine downy hair. His head was small and angular, something like that of a dog and covered with short, black curly hair that hugged the skin tightly. The hands were small, shriveled and covered with hair similar to that on his ears. Young Olson was now becoming almost frightened out of his wits at being alone in the boat with such an unearthly looking being and rowed with all his might. On arriving at the opposite landing he got out of the boat hastily to let out his uncongenial passenger. The stranger arose to leave the boat, but instead of facing about to walk out, he backed and carefully kept his face from view.

The rattled young Olson rowed back home as fast as his arm and oar would take him. The moment he was inside the house, he began to tell his mother about his bizarre adventure. She looked over to him to see if he was serious, and as she did so, her glance fell over into his shoulder and out the window behind him. There, running up a hill close to the house, was the strange boy last seen on the other side of the lake, though he could not possibly have made the return trip anywhere nearly that quickly. The stranger was chasing the Olson's sheep.

Mother and son both made after him, but on arriving at the crest of the hill nobody was to be seen, while the sheep stood down the slope a little way huddled together as if recently chased by a wolf or dog. There was nothing within eighty rods that the stranger could have hid behind. Why they did not notice his strange appearance before starting in the boat, how he got back so quickly and where he disappeared to, was more than the frightened widow and son could have been able to account for and they firmly believe there are still a few left of the old time elf family.

Though Mrs. Olson seemed to think of the strange boy as an elf or fairy-type being, I look at this story through the lens of lycanthropy considering that he returned to chase the family's sheep. After all, what would an elf be doing chasing sheep? And, with the many werewolf tales tracked down by Linda S. Godfrey over in the years in Wisconsin, perhaps this one should be added to the list.

CHAPTER 10
WEREWOLVES OF INDIANA

Indiana's city of Vincennes has some unusual werewolf lore. Part of the reason for this is that it was founded by the French in 1732. Over the years, as area historians gathered local folklore, they found quite a few loup-garou tales. One of the more detailed ones came from an old French woman interviewed in 1935. She told how years ago a strange beast was seen running around a local cemetery. One night, a man named Charles Vatchet had a run-in with the creature, which turned out to be a werewolf:

> One night as Mr. Vatchet was going home, an object having the shape of a wild animal sprang at Mr. Vatchet. He cut the animal with his knife

in his struggle, and the object turned into a man. He gave Mr. Vatchet his name and address (the man was from Evansville), and requested that he should not tell anyone for one year and a day or he would turn back into an animal. When the animals were injured to the extent that brought blood, the charm was broken.

915.—Dusky or Clouded Wolf.

Though this might sound odd, it lines up with other area folklore. In *French Folklife in Old Vincennes*, it is written that:

The main way that [the afflicted] could be released from the spell before serving the stipulated time was for someone to recognize him as a person transformed into an animal and somehow draw blood from the loup-garou. Even when the disenchantment had been performed, both the victim and his rescuer could not mention the incident, even to each other, until the time was up.

Also in Indiana, in Marshall County in 1872, two wolf-like creatures terrorized an area in the vicinity of Devil's Swamp[34] south of Tipton. Not only did livestock go missing, but horrid screams came from out of the darkness. Those who saw the beasts said that they were huge wolves with glowing red eyes.

The Cleveland Plain Dealer reported of another potential werewolf sighting near Sailor, Indiana, on May 1, 1897, which occurred on April 30th:

> Two farmers living near Sailor are considerably aroused over the appearance in the woods of a strange animal which resembles a man. It has been reported for the last two years that a mysterious animal inhabited the woods, but the reports were never credited until yesterday, when Adam Gardner and Ed Swinehart, two well-known farmers, reported that the animal was seen and that shots were fired at it. The men report that the beast walked on its hind feet and had every appearance of a man, save the body was covered with hair. The height was that of an average-sized man. When the animal saw the men approaching it jumped and started for the thick portion of the woods upon its hind legs,

---

[34] As Loren Coleman pointed out in *Mysterious America*, places named in conjunction with the devil usually had long histories of strange events, hence their namesakes.

but afterwards dropped on its hands and disappeared with rabbit-like bounds. Gardner shot at the animal and thinks he hit it, as the animal seemed lamed. A searching party is being organized to hunt for the mysterious animal."

Perhaps they were simply the Werewolves of Vincennes afoot in another county?

SKINWALKERS, WEREWOLVES, AND HELLHOUNDS OF NORTH AMERICA

THE VEGETARIAN WEREWOLF

In *The Hermit of Siskiyou*, a short book by L.W. Musick published in 1896, a bulldog-like werewolf was sighted in California in 1886. In a footnote, the book related the following:

Note 1. A Del Norte Record Correspondent writing from Happy Camp, Siskiyou County, Jan. 2, 1886, discourses as follows:

I do not remember to have seen any reference to the 'Wild Man' which haunts this part of the country, so I shall allude to him briefly. Not a great while since, Mr. Jack Dover, one of our most trustworthy citizens, while hunting saw an object standing one hundred and fifty yards from him picking berries and tender shoots from the bushes.

The thing was of gigantic size; about seven feet high, with a bull dog head, short ears and long hair; it was also furnished with a beard, and was free from hair on such parts of his body as is common among men. Its voice was shrill, or soprano, and very human, like that of a woman in great fear. Mr. Dover could not see its footprints as it walked on hard soil. He aimed his gun at the animal, or whatever it was, but because it was so human would not shoot. The range of the curiosity is between Marble Mountain and the vicinity of Happy Camp. A number of people have seen it and all agree in their descriptions except some make it taller than others. It is apparently herbivorous and makes winter quarters in some caves of Marble Mountain.

COWBOYS & DOGMEN

**F.N. WILSON ILLUSTRATION FROM
"INDIAN DAYS OF THE LONG AGO" C. 1915.**

CHAPTER II
CRIMSON COYOTE

Far in the north in the late 1880s once lived a hermit by the name of Red Morgan in a cabin in Saskatchewan, Canada. According to legend, Red Morgan was a werewolf of a rather unique sort who could turn himself into a red coyote. In 1887, this fearsome red coyote was the terror of all the miners in Saskatchewan. The beast wasn't just killing animals, but men, women, and children were all found with their throats slashed open. Eventually, rumors began to spread that the red coyote wasn't just an animal, but a were-coyote.

What's more, the tracks of the beast always disappeared into a mountain located behind the cabin of Red Morgan, the old miner turned hermit. One night, a young miner happened to spot the vicious red coyote. Ed Bodin recounted what happened next in his book *Scare Me! A Symposium on Ghosts and Black Magic*:

> Then one moonlit night a young miner saw the beast. It was slinking behind a hill less than a half mile away. The young miner reached for his rifle. But he had no bullets although plenty of powder. He must get a bullet somehow, no matter what the cost. Lives were at stake. The only metal he had was gold. Gold nuggets. Quickly he fashioned a bullet and started after the beast.
>
> The snow was light, so he tracked it for several miles. Then he saw it. And the beast saw him at the same time. Never before had a coyote turned on a man like this, for the animal charged him with all the fury of its wolf ancestors. Would the golden bullet stop it?
>
> The beast was almost upon him. He took careful aim. The rifle shot echoed throughout the valley. The coyote reared. It stopped but didn't fall. Wounded, it turned and ran to the forest nearby. The young miner followed the blood spots, but the wind covered most of the tracks and they were lost in the denseness of the woods. Undoubtedly the beast would drop sooner or later, so the miner returned and told his friends of the good news.
>
> Two days later the miners were gathered in the general store. They were talking about the red coyote. It had not been seen for the past two nights. Then a native came in. "Did you hear

the news?" he said. "Red Morgan was found dead in his cabin—a bullet hole in his chest."

"When did it happen?"

"Don't know, but this morning young Bradley stopped at Red Morgan's to bring him the newspaper and found Morgan dead on the floor." But here is the strange discovery that no one has ever been able to explain. The doctor found a gold bullet in Morgan's body! And from that day on no one ever saw the red coyote again.[35]

A miner killing a werewolf with a golden bullet? It doesn't get much cooler than that, which means that it was probably made up. The story was related in 1940 to Ed Bodin by a mining engineer living in New York who had lived in Saskatchewan as a boy during the time of the fearsome killings. According

---

[35] Bodin, *Scare Me!*, pp.79-80.

to the man, his mother and father wouldn't even let him out of the house after dark for fear of the beast. Bodin then immortalized the tale in his book, and it has been recounted ever since.

Sources:

Bodin, Ed. *Scare Me! A Symposium on Ghosts and Black Magic*. New York: Orlin Tremaine Company, 1940.

CANADA'S OTHER WOLFMAN

Though not nearly as interesting as the story just related, I would be remiss in not also passing along this other Canadian "werewolf" tale. It was published in the *Victoria Advocate* on September 17, 1922:

FIND FREAK WOLF-MAN
Creature Living With Indians Walks on Hands and Feet
Is Wolf In All Except Form and Is Said to be About 70 Years Old— Subsists on Meat In Kennel.

Victoria, B.C.—A strange wolf-man has been discovered living with the Hesqualt Indians on the west coast of Vancouver island, B. C., Canada. So isolated is this island that no effort has been made to give scientific attention to this strange creature till quite recently. The wolf-man is called Kilra-ith-ka, which means wolf-man in the Indian tongue. He is a wolf in all except form and is said to be about seventy years old.

He resembles an old man walking on his hands and feet; he has never walked after the human fashion. He cannot make any human sound, but growls like a wolf. He eats like one and where human beings have eye teeth he has canine fangs. When the wolf-man sits erect he is four feet and a half-inch [sic] tall. He subsists on raw or cooked meat and lives in a kennel in the rear of the house of a keeper appointed by the tribe. The keeper feeds him and keeps clothes on him as much as possible, and except for occasional disrobings, Kilra-ith-ka is fairly tractable and accepts semidomestication which is about his only human trait. The ethnologist who investigated the man learned from the Indians that in the days when the wolf-man was born wolves were very plentiful on the coast and at times attacked people. Whether this is the cause of the man's animal-like state the fact remains that Kilra-ith-ka is a wolf in everything except form. He is regarded with great awe by his tribesmen, a common thing among primitive people, who very often venerate any human being different from the ordinary.

CHAPTER 12
CURSE OF THE CAT PEOPLE

In 1942 was released Val Lewton's now-classic horror film *Cat People*. Although I'm sure many just assume it was inspired by the success of *The Wolf Man* the previous year, there are indeed stories of were-cats just as there are of werewolves. Such accounts take place the world over, and some of the more notable ones come from the ancient Aztecs of Mexico, who believed in were-panthers.

Coincidentally, the story we are about to cover took place in the town of Mexico, Missouri, and was reported in the *Alton Telegraph* on December 13, 1883:

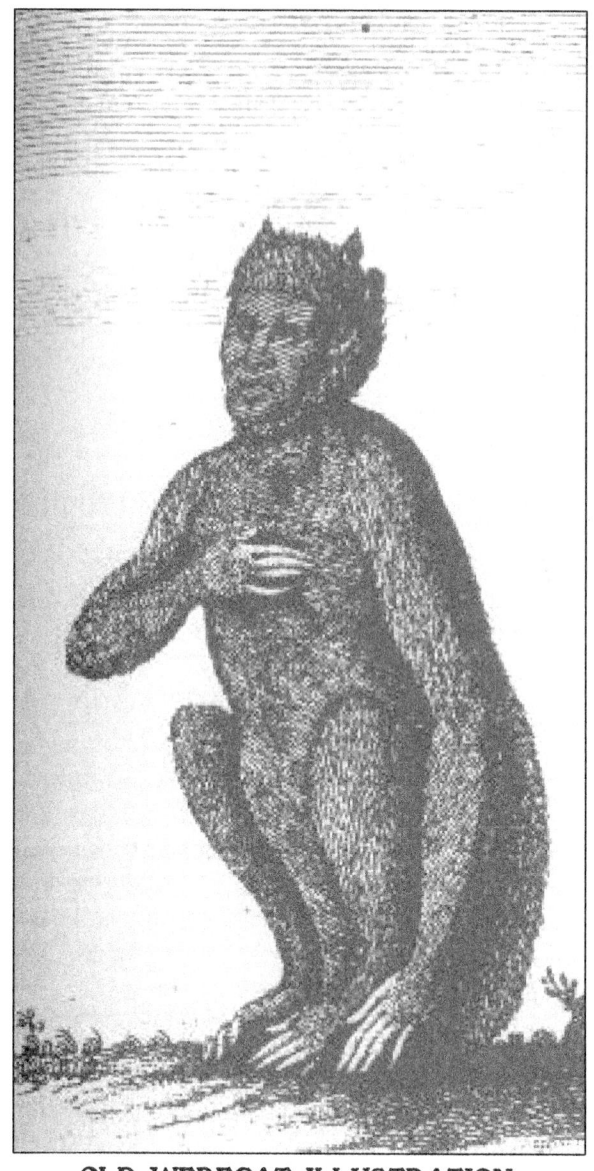

OLD WERECAT ILLUSTRATION.

SKINWALKERS, WEREWOLVES, AND HELLHOUNDS OF NORTH AMERICA

A WHAT IS IT?
A Strange Apparition Frightens the People of a Missouri Town.

Mexico, Mo., Dec. 10.—The neighborhood of Hopewell Church, near this city, is much excited over the appearance in the locality of a strange creature, which is thought by the credulous to be a ghost, and which is a puzzle at least to the most skeptical. The apparition is simply that of a lean monster man, between eight and ten feet in height, wearing a long cloak, and going about with his head bowed in an abstracted way, but occasionally glaring at those it meets with small, glittering eyes, said to resemble those of a cat or some wild beast. The negroes believe the apparition to be a ghost, the white people do not know what to say. There appears little doubt, whatever the creature may be, that it has actually been seen a number of times. The school at Hopewell church is about to be abandoned because of fear of the monster, and even sturdy farmers go about armed, in apprehension of it. John Creary, a well-known old resident, declares that Saturday afternoon as he was returning from Mexico to his home he had a good view of the queer being, who was about fifty yards ahead of him, walking in a leisurely way along the middle of the big road, in mud almost knee-deep, his head still and his long black cloak flowing in the breeze at once, and in the twinkling of an eye, he disappeared in the thick woods as mysteriously as he came upon the scene. Mr. Creary says for the first time in all his life, although a soldier under Gen. Grant, he was really frightened, and it was all he could do to control the horse he was riding, so great seemed its fear of the object.

Mr. Cyrus Haggert and wife, who were returning from church Thanksgiving eve, were surprised by the monster's peering with its cat-like-eyes into their buggy and leaning against it, almost crushing the vehicle. The lady has not yet, it is said, recovered from the shock occasioned by the sight of the monster.

As you can see, the man-thing described in this story was more of a spook in the vein of beings like Spring-Heeled Jack, but the detail of the cat-like eyes certainly lingers.

CHAPTER 13
THE BEAR MAN

In this book's introduction was briefly mentioned the myth of the berserker, Viking men who adorned themselves with the pelts of a bear and then went into battle with an absolute frenzy. In this case, berserker or not, we have an article purporting to tell of a creature with a bear's body and a man's head published in the *Duluth News-Tribune* on December 3, 1906. Make of it what you will...

> These are sleepless nights in Upland. A wild creature, which, according to eye-witnesses, is half man, half beast, has literally terrorized the borough. No one ventures out after dark without a club or lantern, and the more determined carry guns. The perturbation of the residents is such that they are ready to shoot first

and investigate afterward. This, they say, is the only way to tackle such weird game.

As no one knows whether the thing is human or not, residents speak of the creature as "it." Tales told by those who have been cuffed and chased by "it" are more uncanny than "The Headless Horseman of Sleepy Hollow," or "The Hound of the Baskervilles." Judging by the descriptions gathered yesterday from a score of persons who saw the creature it has a body like a bear and a head like a man. Its eyes glitter like hot coals; its voice is sepulchral and changes rapidly to thunderous tones, and it can run like the wind.

Aroused by the actions of the creature, which chased their sisters and sweethearts, the football team of the Upland high school and a number of citizens armed with clubs and guns, descended last night upon the woods at Summit Avenue intending to surprise the thing in its lair. The searchers spread out in a circle and then closed in. In the heart of the woods they found a small bonfire and the remains of a meal, but the mysterious creature had disappeared. Among those who have been chased by "it" are Albert Murphy and Horace Kemmerle. Murphy said, "The thing jumped out in front of me as I was walking Summit Street. From the quick glance that I took the thing looked like a polar bear with a man's head.

I did not stop to investigate, but ran home as fast as I could. The thing followed me for a short distance and then suddenly disappeared. Walter Dunkirk said it chased him while he was walking along Concord Avenue. "It looked like a sheep and walked like a man," he said. "It struck me on the neck and I felt as if I had been struck by a thousand needles." Horace Kemmerle, who was chased along Providence Avenue by "it" said that the creature looked like a sheep with a man's head. He didn't stop to make a minute examination. Policeman Harry

Beals, who is the entire force of Upland, said yesterday "this thing has been seen on Summit and Providence avenues and those places are on the beats of the Chester police. I have been keeping my eyes open, however, and the first glimpse I get at this thing I'll run it down anyhow."

CHAPTER 14
WEREWOLF WOMAN OF TALBOT COUNTY

Georgia's best known werewolf tale is likely that of the poor "werewolf girl" of Talbot County,[36] Isabella Burt. While it can be proven that Burt was indeed a real woman who was born in the 1840s and lived in the area with her mother and three sisters, it's uncertain whether the tales of her werewolf-like deeds are the truth or gross exaggerations.

Variations of the story attest that Isabella didn't begin to resemble a werewolf until after coming home from a trip to Europe, while others state that

---

[36] An odd coincidence in terms of the name, I know, since Lon Chaney Jr.'s character was named Larry Talbot in *The Wolf Man*. However, the county, created in 1827, was named for the deceased Georgia governor Matthew Talbot.

Isabella inherited her wolf-like looks from her late father. But, as you can see in the picture, the real Isabella wasn't all that wolfish looking. However, Isabella isn't smiling in this picture, either, and if lore is to be believed, her most distinctive feature was her sharp, animal-like teeth. In *Georgia Ghosts*, Nancy Roberts described the girl's teeth as looking like they had been "shaped with a file" and were "pointed." Supposedly, the teeth were so noticeable and distracting that the wealthy Mrs. Burt consulted a dentist as to whether or not anything could be done for her daughter's frightening teeth. However, the dentist said that nothing could be done for the girl's unfortunate condition and that she'd have to live with it.

But the pointed teeth were the least of poor Isabella's problems. Isabella also suffered from insomnia, and on some nights would leave home in the middle of the night to wander the woods. Around the same time that Isabella's insomnia kicked into overdrive, farmers began reporting attacks on their livestock. This went on for an unknown duration of time, but the story came to a head in a similar fashion to the movie *The Wolf Man*, which, if you'll recall, had Larry Talbot's father being the one to kill his son.

In this case, Isabella's sister, Sarah, watched Isabella slip into the night and followed her. Unbeknownst to them both, their mother also followed her daughters into the night, carrying a gun for protection. On this same night, a group of hunters was also out to get the animal attacking their livestock.

There are several variations as to what happened that night. Some are far-out enough to suggest that the hunters actually saw a werewolf and used silver bullets to shoot at it. Other, more down-to-earth variations of the story say that Isabella was simply spotted clutching a knife as she leered at some livestock in a sheep pasture in the distance. Mrs. Burt came on the scene just as Isabella was about to pounce and called at her to stop. Supposedly, Isabella turned to look at her and snarled like an animal. Then, one of the hunters shot Isabella. Or so that story goes. Another more interesting version goes that the men shot a wolf in the foot, and that Mrs. Burt later found Isabella, minus a hand, lying in a pool of her own blood.

In all versions, Isabella survives the gunshot wound and is sent off to Europe. Though said to be visiting relatives, in reality, she was being treated by a doctor in Paris for lycanthropy, the condition which causes a human being to believe that they are a wolf. And, considering that Isabella was said to have a keen interest in the occult and the supernatural, she might well have suffered from this affliction.

To cap off the story, while Isabella was away, the attacks on livestock ceased. When she returned, cured of her mental affliction, she lived out a normal life, passing away at the age of 70 in 1911. Upon her death, supposedly some of the area residents objected to her receiving a Christian burial, what with her having been a werewolf and all. However, cooler heads prevailed, and Isabella was buried in the local cemetery just like everyone else. Today, allegedly, her ghost can be seen roaming Ownes and Holmes Cemetery, where she is buried.

ISABELLA BURT'S GRAVE.

Again, it's unknown how much of Isabella's story is true, and even modern-day relatives still debate what really happened. I think the real key in understanding this story is, when did it actually start to circulate? If it came about after the release of *The Wolf Man* in 1941, I would have to guess it was mostly fabricated based on the fact that it took place in Talbot County. Furthermore, the story is quite similar to *She-Wolf of London*, a little-known Universal horror film from 1946. In that decidedly disappointing flick, the titular character is just a sleep-walker who thinks she's a wolf, much like the girl in this story. And, again, the climax of Isabella's own story reeks of *The Wolf Man*, where Larry Talbot's father finds his son in wolf form out in the woods. Ultimately we'll have to be content with wondering if art imitated life, or if it was the other way around.

Sources:

Roberts, Nancy. *Georgia Ghosts*. Blair, 1997.

Weatherly, David. *Peach State Monsters: Cryptids & Legends of Georgia*. Eerie Lights Publishing, 2021.

COWBOYS & DOGMEN

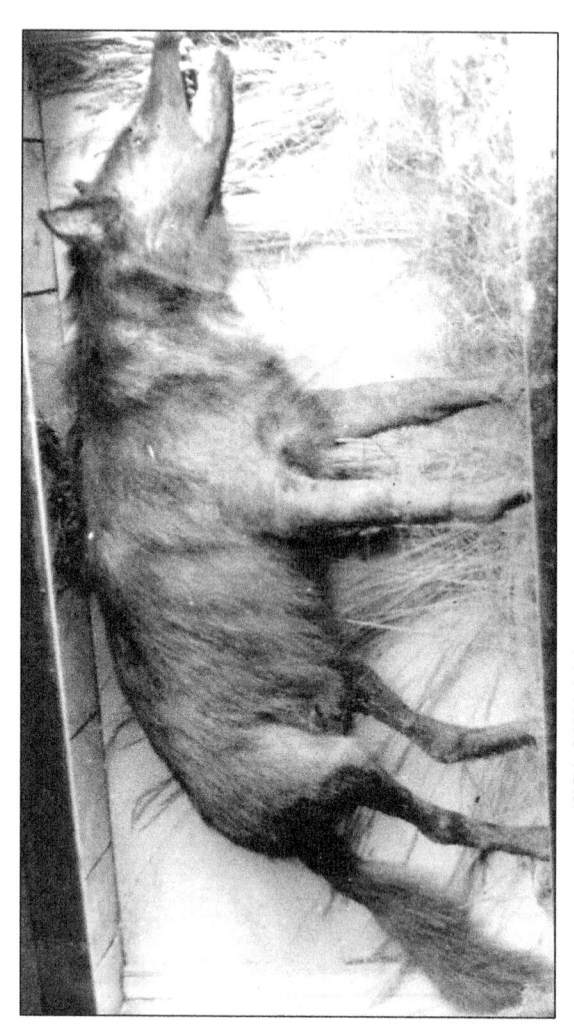

THE RINGDOCUS AKA THE SHUNKA WARAK'IN

CHAPTER 15
SAGA OF THE SHUNKA WARAK'IN

It's debatable whether or not this case should be included in this book, as it presents another cryptid canine with scant ties to the supernatural—those being that, upon being shot, it cried like a human being (and for that reason, some Native Americans revered it). If anything, the animal is most comparable to the Dog Eater covered in an earlier chapter. The creature was called the *shunka warak'in*—literally meaning "carries off dogs"—by Iowa's Ioway tribe. The hyena-like beast would sneak into their camps at night and—as the name implies—kill and carry away dogs.

Researcher Lance M. Foster managed to find some of the older accounts of the shunka warak'in thanks to notes taken on the subject by Alanson Skinner. In the early 1900s, Skinner heard the tales of the strange animal firsthand from the Ioway Indians. The tales came from Chief David Tohee and Joseph Springer and told of the tribesmen killing a strange animal and keeping its skin. Skinner wrote the following in his "Ethnology of the Ioway Indians," published in 1926:

> One time the people began to miss their dogs. Every morning a few were gone, and no one knew the cause. Some thought it the work of an enemy, so the young men got up a war party and hid themselves so as to surprise and kill the nightly visitor. It turned out to be a strange animal, different from anything they had ever seen before. They named it "Carrying-off-dogs," but it is very like the animal the white people keep in their shows today and call hyena. When it entered the camp, the young warriors attacked it just as if it was a person. Again and again they shot at this creature, and could not kill it, but after following it a day and a half they at last succeeded in putting it to death. When it died, it cried just like a human being. When they heard this, and thought of the hard time they had in killing it, they decided that it must be a creature of great power. So they skinned it, and painted its hide, and later placed the hide in with the other powerful objects in the war bundle, to wear in battle across the shoulder to turn away flying bullets and arrows. But before the hide was put in the bundle, a big dance was held.

Immediately afterward a party set out and were very successful, as they killed a number of enemies, returning with many scalps. (Skinner 1926: 211-212).[37]

Unfortunately, the hide of this animal cannot be found today. However, in Montana, one of the creatures was killed in 1886 by Israel Hutchins. The Hutchins family arrived in the Madison River Valley in Montana by covered wagon in the 1880s. Hutchins had been searching for gold all across the U.S. until finally his wife put a stop to it and insisted that the family finally settle down. There the Mormon settlers established a model ranch, located about 40 miles from the town of Ennis. Eventually, they would be the recipient of a very strange visitor.

The man's grandson, Ross Hutchins, wrote about the incident many years later in his book *Trails to Nature's Mysteries: The Life of a Working Naturalist.*

Strange things often happened in the wild area where our ranch was located. One winter morning my grandfather was aroused by the barking of dogs. He discovered that a wolf-like beast of dark color was chasing my grandmother's geese. He fired his gun at the animal but missed. It ran off down the river, but

---

[37] Foster, "Shunka Warak'in: A Mystery in Plain Sight," http://paranormalmontana.blogspot.com/2009/03/shunka-warakin.html

several mornings later it was seen again at about dawn. It was seen several more times at the home ranch as well as at other ranches ten or fifteen miles down the valley. Whatever it was, it was a great traveler...

Those who got a good look at the beast described it as being nearly black and having high shoulders and a back that sloped downward like a hyena. Then one morning in late January, my grandfather was alerted by the dogs, and this time he was able to kill it. Just what the animal was is still an open question. After being killed, it was donated to a man named [Joseph] Sherwood who kept a combination grocery and museum at Henry Lake in Idaho.[38] It was mounted and displayed there for many years. He called it "ringdocus."[39]

And there the ringdocus sat for nearly 100 years. Then, in the 1980s, it mysteriously disappeared. In 1987, a book entitled *Just West of Yellowstone: A Guide to Exploring and Camping* was written by a landscape architect named Rae Ellen Moore. She wrote of seeing the mount of a strange hyena-like animal in a small museum in Henry's Lake, Idaho. Lucky for us, shunka warak'in researcher Lance M. Foster read the book and connected the dots.

---

[38] Other sources say Hutchins traded it to Sherwood for a cow.
[39] Hutchins, *Trails to Nature's Mysteries*, p.50.

SKINWALKERS, WEREWOLVES, AND HELLHOUNDS OF NORTH AMERICA

Foster did some digging and was disappointed to learn that the museum had closed down, and no one knew what had happened to the taxidermy collection there either. Around this time, Foster also drew parallels between the shunka warak'in of Iowa and the Ringdocus of Montana. He wrote to famed cryptozoologist Loren Coleman about the strange creatures. Coleman, in turn, wrote about it in his book *Cryptozoology A to Z* in 1999, reigniting interest in the old cryptid and its missing mount.

BOROPHAGUS BY CHARLES KNIGHT C.1902.

Coleman and Foster both speculated that it could have been a type of prehistoric hyena. Coleman theorized that it could be a Borophagus, a type of hyena-like dog from the Pleistocene epoch. The Borophagus had powerful, bone-crushing jaws and was essentially built like a coyote on steroids. Scientists speculated that it was probably a scavenger just like modern hyenas.

Together Foster and Coleman did their best to find the old taxidermy mount, even getting confirmation that the Idaho Museum of Natural History did indeed acquire the Sherwood mounts from Henry's Lake, Idaho. However, Coleman and Foster were beaten to the rediscovery by Jack Kirby, the grandson of Israel Hutchins. Kirby had managed to find the mount in the Idaho Museum of Natural History and had even got them to loan it to him.

One of the first things Kirby did was take the mount to the grave of his grandfather, to tell him that they had brought the mystery creature home. The discovery at long last also managed to confirm the exact dimensions of the animal. An article on the discovery reported that, "It measures 48 inches from the tip of its snout to its rump, not including the tail, and stands from 27 to 28 inches high at the shoulder."[40]

In May of 2007, the specimen was put on display in the recently reopened Madison Valley History Museum. When asked to submit the creature for DNA testing to determine what it was, Kirby declined, wanting to let the mystery linger. His remark: "Do we want to know?"

Soon after the animal's return to Montana, the Island Park Historical Society of Idaho expressed

---

40 www.bozemandailychronicle.com/news/mystery-monster-returns-home-after-years/article_461c6958-ca1e-5f57-bee9-a3c11b0a18a6.html

concern that they may never get the old mount back. The group wished to have it displayed at the John Sack cabin in Island Park.

Further confusing the matter is an alternate story that claims the beast was really shot and killed in Idaho at a spot called Mack's Inn on the banks of the Snake River. Harold Bishop, a Mack's Inn resident, was researching the animal for a scout project. Over the course of his research, he interviewed a man named Pete Marx, who insisted the animal was shot by a range rider named Heini Schooster with a lever-action .32 special.

As is typical of cryptids, the ringdocus just continues to confuse rather than enlighten...

Sources:

Foster, Lance. "Shunka Warak'in: A Mystery in Plain Sight." Paranormal Montana. (March 3, 2009) http://paranormalmontana.blogspot.com/2009/03/shunka-warakin.html

Hutchins, Ross. *Trails to Nature's Mysteries.* New York, NY: Dodd, Mead & Company, 1977.

Williams, Walt. "Mystery monster returns home after 121 years." *Bozeman Daily Chronicle.* (November 14, 2007)
https://www.bozemandailychronicle.com/news/mystery-monster-returns-home-after-years/article_461c6958-ea1e-5f57-bee9-a3c11b0a18a6.html

IDAHO'S WEREWOLF

Apart from the Shunka Warak'in, Idaho has one other notable werewolf story, though it sounds to be nothing more than an urban legend. Within the Rose Hill Cemetery in Idaho Falls can be found two graves side by side, one sporting the surname Were and the other Wolff. Probably, someone simply made up a legend based upon the odd coincidence. The story went that at an unspecified time in Idaho Fall's past, a series of grisly murders erupted. The bodies of several residents were found and appeared to have been mutilated by a wild animal. But why would the animal attack humans when there was plenty of wild game to attack instead? That was the townsfolk's first clue that it may be a werewolf. Their suspicions turned out to be right, and soon an angry mob of villagers managed to track down and kill the beast... somehow. However they killed the alleged werewolf, to be extra careful, they cut the body in two and buried each half in a separate grave. This, they felt, would keep it from ever resurrecting. In true urban legend style, not long after this, both graves were found to have been exhumed. Furthermore, a bite was taken out of the headstone reading Wolff.

CHAPTER 16
HOUNDS OF HEAVEN AND HELL

The Hellhound legend is one that spans across nations, each with its unique variations. The most exciting species of Hellhound, if they could be called such, hails from Mexico and South America. This is because not only are there three distinct varieties of the evil black dogs from Hell below, but they have an opposing number in the form of a white dog from Heaven above. Whether back or white,[41] Latin America's spectral dogs are known as the Cadejo. Tales of the dogs range from as far south as Nicaragua up to Chiapas, Mexico.

---

[41] In some legends, it is the white dogs that are bad, and the black that are good, but the opposite version is the more widespread one.

DREADED BLACK CADEJO.

As stated before, there are three distinct varieties of the evil kind. Some have hooves like a deer, which has piqued the interests of the cryptozoological community on the off chance that perhaps the dogs are flesh and blood cryptids rather than spiritual manifestations. Along with the deer-like hooves comes the trot of a deer as opposed to that of a typical dog. Sometimes, a glowing chain may be glimpsed around their necks. In fact, it may be from this chain, called the *cadena*, that the Cadejo gets its name.

The Cadejo are said to be larger than average dogs (sometimes as big as a cow, they say), and often have more fur as well. The first variety of Cadejo isn't terribly different from Old Shuck or other hellhounds as it reeks of sulfur and sports red

SKINWALKERS, WEREWOLVES, AND HELLHOUNDS OF NORTH AMERICA

eyes.[42] It is thought of as a pure manifestation of evil, maybe even the form of the very devil at times. As such, one can usually ward it off with the sign of the cross. Oftentimes when these creatures appear, they are accompanied by visions of hell, warning the witness to repent of their sins. As a precaution, it is said that one should stand firmly with their feet together lest the Cadejo run between one's legs and whisk them off to the underworld. That said, the Cadejo can also freeze its victims in place when one is unfortunate enough to look it in the eye.

The second variety of Cadejo is evil physically incarnate. Whereas the previous version serves more as a bad omen, the second variety is a flesh and blood being that kills its victims. Nor do signs of the cross ward them off. Supposedly, sightings of these devil dogs begin with it taunting its prey, almost as if to feed upon their fear. When the desired level of terror is reached, they will then rip their victim to pieces. They are said to be unstoppable unless divine intervention occurs, which can also include the good, White Cadejo.

The third Cadejo is a hybrid canine, a mixture of the second type of Cadejo just described and a normal dog. It is the lesser of the three evils and can be killed. However, this version still reeks of silly folklore in the sense that it doesn't bite its victims but pecks them to death with its snout! However, in doing so, they also drive their victim

---

[42] Rather than sulfur, others say it stinks like a goat or urine. And as for another variation, sometimes the eyes are purple rather than red.

mad, it is said. Unlike the second iteration, this hybrid can be warded off by the sign of the cross. And, again in the vein of silly folklore, one can spit in their hand and hold it out to the Cadejo. If it licks it, all is well. But if not, it plans to fight you. When it is killed, just like a vampire in an old movie, its body will decompose rapidly and disappear within minutes. Thereafter, it is said nothing will ever grow on that spot of earth again.[43]

Finally we can move on to the last variety, that being the fluffy white-furred, blue-eyed Cadejo that fights for the side of good. These benevolent canines most often appear at night to protect travelers on their journeys or even to guide them to their destination when they become lost. As alluded to earlier, this White Cadejo is the only creature capable of killing the second variety of Black Cadejo.[44] Oddly, the White Cadejo doesn't eat meat and only gorges itself upon small bell-like flowers that grow at the rims of volcanos and mountains in Southern Mexico.

The most famous folktale of the White Cadejo centered on a man identified only as Juan and was said to take place in the early 20th Century near Los Arcos, Guatemala. As it was, Juan worked late and was away all day, leaving his wife and young children at home unprotected. When Juan would arrive home at midnight, he would always see a

---

[43] The area is also said to smell terrible for several days as well.
[44] That said, the White Cadejo is supposedly incapable of defeating the first type of purely spectral cadejo.

large white dog near his home. Whenever he attempted to pet it, it would run away into the foliage. One day, Juan followed it into the country. Upon finally meeting up with the canine, it began to speak to him, explaining that it had been sent to watch over his family. However, that time was now over, as Juan was now capable of protecting his own family the dog said. Instead of disappearing into a ghostly mist or ascending into Heaven, the white dog fell limp and died. Juan buried him and thus ends the tail.

Sources:

Bitto, Robert. "Cadejos: Gigantic Dogs of Good & Evil." Mexico Unexplained. (August 13, 2017)
https://mexicounexplained.com/cadejos-gigantic-dogs-good-evil/

SUNSET ROUTE. CASTLE CANYON. NEAR DEVILS RIVER. TEXAS.

CHAPTER 17
LOBO GIRL OF DEVIL RIVER

In the Autumn of 1834, Mollie Dent mailed her parents in Georgia a rather ominous letter from Texas, where she and her husband had just moved. The short letter read:

Dear Mother,
The Devil has a river in Texas that is all his own
and it is made only for those who are grown.
Yours with love
Mollie

The rather ominous and cryptic letter referred to Devil's River, located in southwestern Texas. Mollie and her husband, John Dent, had recently moved there from Georgia, and not under the best of circumstances, either. John had been a trapper along Georgia's Chickamauga River along with a partner, Will Marlo. In 1833, John met Mollie Pertul, the daughter of some local farmers, and fell in love. Planning to marry Mollie, John needed to up his income and so quit splitting his profits with Marlo. Things escalated into a violent confrontation, and John ended up stabbing his old partner to death.

That is the reason that John and Mollie, now his wife, fled to Texas in 1834, where John began trapping beavers along the Devil's River.[45] The two lived in a brush cabin not too far away from a place now known as Carrizo Springs in the vicinity of Lake Espontosa. The area was a dangerous place, too, and a group of settlers was massacred by a tribe of Commanche, who threw the bodies of their victims into Lake Espontosa.

Eventually, John and Mollie would themselves fall victim to a massacre, but not from the Commanche... By May of 1835, Mollie learned that she was pregnant, and the couple, fearful of the nearby Commanche, decided to move to a better

---

[45] An alternate flourish to this story goes that Mollie Pertul was left behind by John when he went on the run, waiting for his return. Meanwhile, her parents just hoped Mollie would give up on the fugitive John and find a better suitor. Then, a year to the day that John killed his partner in April of 1834, Mollie vanished. Not only did she vanish, she had gone out to milk the cows, and in a milk pale was found the same bloodstained Bowie knife that had killed Marlo. Perhaps the bloody knife was meant to trick Mollie's parents into thinking she had been killed so they wouldn't look for her?

area known as Beaver Lake along the Devil's River. John built a new cabin and the family settled in. Then, on a dark and stormy night, Mollie began to go into labor. But, it was a troublesome birth, and not knowing what to do, John rode to get help from a Mexican goat ranch in Pecos Canyon. Some of the men agreed to ride back with John to his cabin, but as they mounted their horses, a lightning strike literally struck John dead.

POSTCARD OF DEVIL'S RIVER.

The Mexican farmers set out to find John's poor widow but didn't arrive until sunrise the next morning. Ominously, wolf prints surrounded the cabin. Inside, to their shock, they found Mrs. Dent dead. From the best that they could tell, she had been killed by wolves as her body bore traces of bite wounds. As for the poor baby, they could only guess that it had been devoured by the wolves. Only it wasn't.

Ten years later, at San Felipe Springs in 1845, a boy sighted a wolf pack attacking a herd of goats. That in and of itself wasn't unusual for the time. What was unusual was another form within the wolf pack that he described as "a creature, with long hair covering its features, that looked like a naked girl." Though the story was ridiculed by those that heard it, that didn't stop them from spreading it around. It was fascinating conversation, after all. A year later, a woman from San Felipe also saw the feral girl in the company of two large wolves. Together the three were feasting upon a freshly killed goat. When the woman approached, the wolves and the girl took notice and scampered away. The girl also ran on all fours for a bit before rising up on two feet like a normal human would.

With two people having seen the feral girl, area residents began to keep a sharp eye out for the Lobo Girl of Devil's River as she was beginning to be known. The Apache, too, took notice of a child's footprints and handprints mixed in with the tracks of the wolves in sandy places along the river. Mexican vaqueros (cowboys) decided to search out the poor girl, and within three days managed to sight her running with her pack along Espontosa Lake.[46] The vaqueros managed to catch the girl when they cornered her in a canyon. Having been raised by wolves her whole life, she was naturally terrified of the men and bit and clawed at them

---

[46] In the version of the tale published in *Straight Texas*, a folklore collection printed in 1937, it was apparently only two cowboys who cornered the girl in the canyon.

when they approached her. The men had to resort to lassoing the girl, and as they tied her up, they reported that she let out unearthly howls that sounded like a cross between human and animal. What was described as a "monster he-wolf" came to her rescue and attacked the men. One of the vaqueros swiftly shot it dead, and the poor lobo girl fainted.

FERAL CHILD PLAYING WITH WOLVES.

Able to examine her still form for the first time, they took note that although she was covered in unkempt hair, she was indeed human. They also took note of her well-muscled arms and legs, developed over time from running on all fours. (The men would later observe that she seemed more adept at maneuvering on all fours as opposed to on two legs like a normal human.)

The lobo girl was put on a horse and taken to a nearby ranch, where she was placed in a shack. When the men offered her a covering for her naked body, she either refused it or didn't know what it was for. The same was true of speech, for she couldn't utter words or syllables like her captors, only guttural growls. Not knowing what else to do, they left her alone.

That night, she howled into the darkness and her distant pack answered her. Soon the ranch was beset upon by her rescuing wolfpack, which attacked goats, cattle, and other livestock. The cowboys did their best to fend them off with guns, but in the chaos, the lobo girl tore the planks off of a boarded-up window and escaped back into the wild.

Devils River Natural Dam Resort near Del Rio, Tex.
O. F. Wyrick, Prop.

After that, no further attempts to capture the girl were made. However, the lobo girl was still sighted semi often. And it would be at this point that the sightings would take on a more fantastical, some might even say supernatural, nature. A surveying party looking for an alternate route to El Paso were riding down the Rio Grande in 1852 when they sighted the lobo woman. This time, she was suckling two wolf cubs! When she saw the men, she grabbed the cubs and sprinted into the wilderness at such a rapid gait that not even the horsemen could follow her. One version of the account, possibly from a Texas folklore collection published in 1936, stated, "In an instant she was upon her feet, a whelp under each arm, dashing into the breaks at a rate no horse could follow." Into the 1860s, sightings became infrequent, though soldiers at Camp Hudson claimed they could hear her inhuman howls in the dark of night.

Though it sounds like folklore, the saga of the lobo woman of Devil's River could be true, as tales from antiquity of orphaned children being raised by wolves are quite common. And though she was never really a werewolf, the lobo woman did eventually become a ghost.

As late as 1974, while out hunting for wild pigs (or, javalinas as they are known), a hunter named Jim Marshall and two friends sighted the lobo woman long after she should have been dead. They were camped along Devil's River and had been hunting for four days. That night, when one of the men went to gather some firewood, he returned to camp with a face as white as death. Marshall asked his friend what he had seen, and he replied that it would be better if they saw it for themselves. The two men followed their friend down a trail to the water's edge as he described the strange apparition he had seen, which looked like a young girl. Upon reaching the spot, the apparition was still there. The men later said,

> The only way I can describe it is that it appeared to be a girl, a real skinny girl, with long hair and wild eyes. Even in the darkness we could see her. It was like she was in a haze, a kind of foggy mist, standing there partly bent over, digging into an ant mound. Suddenly whatever we were seeing was gone. I don't know if it vanished or just moved quickly into the brush."[47]

Supposedly, the three men returned to camp, packed up their things, and left as quick as they could.

Sources:

"Was orphan girl really raised by wolves?" Hays Free Press (February 5, 2016).
https://haysfreepress.com/2016/02/05/was-orphan-girl-really-raised-by-wolves/

Humphreys, Gary. "The Wolf Girl of Devil's River." Texas Escapes (April 4, 2011).
http://www.texasescapes.com/TexasFolklore/Wolf-Girl-of-Devils-River.htm

Murray, Earl. *Ghosts of the Old West*. Dorset Press, 1988.

---

[47] Murray, *Ghosts of the Old West*, p.124.

CHAPTER 18
RATON'S WERERAT

The following will undoubtedly be one of the weirdest, meandering werewolf tales you've ever heard. It begins in the small New Mexico settlement of Raton sometime in the mid-1800s. During that time, Raton—which allegedly means rat—ironically was said to be plagued by a gigantic rat. The beastly vermin was said to be the size of a large dog and began killing livestock in the area. For a time, only animals were attacked until one night a child was killed. Hunters followed a bloody trail that led to a hole in the ground, not unlike that of a rat's, only bigger.

One night, a coal miner heard something gnawing at his door. He lit a kerosine lamp and went to check, only whatever it was had disappeared, leaving behind bite marks on the door. Then, the man noticed that the trapdoor to his cellar had been pulled from its hinges. The man walked down the steps of his cellar to investigate and was apparently the first to lay eyes on the black, dog-sized rat monster. The man didn't have a gun on him at the time and fled. Word of the incident spread, and the town became on edge over the rat monster.

RATON, NEW MEXICO.

Night watchmen began to take turns looking for the monster, which only appeared at night. Worse yet, the Goblin Rat—as it was now known—was beginning to raid the local cemetery, exhuming bodies which it would then devour! Things escalated further when at least two of the nightwatchmen disappeared, presumably taken away by the Goblin Rat. Priests came and recited prayers at locations where the beast was seen and eventually it disappeared. Years passed without incident until a local handyman named Cleto Sotero stumbled upon the rat monster. Sotero lived from job to job and usually wasted his paychecks on wine. After one job, Sotero got so drunk that he allegedly wandered into a hole in a hillside to sleep off his drunken bender. As it turned out, the hole was the abode of the Goblin Rat. As Sotero wallowed around in the giant rat's nest, the Goblin Rat eventually took notice of its unwanted visitor and a fight broke out. After that night, it was a long time before Sotero resurfaced...

Shortly after Sotero disappeared, livestock again turned up dead, killed by a vicious predator. The town whispered that the Goblin Rat was back, until one man saw the monster behind the attacks, and it wasn't the Goblin Rat of old. One night, a man happened to witness an abnormally large wolf roaming the wilds of Raton, carrying a fresh kill in its jaws. The man fired a pistol at the beast. To his utter shock, it stood up on two legs like a man and bounded off into the night.

At first, people simply thought the witness was crazy, but then a couple was attacked by the same creature a few nights later. Returning from Cimmaron by wagon, the couple noticed something behind them spooking their horse. Eventually, the horse became so frightened it took off in a dead run. The wagon hit a rock and crashed, throwing the couple from it. The man and his wife scuttled back to the toppled wagon and hid behind it as they observed a huge wolf tear their horse apart. Towards the end of the attack, it stood up on two legs and then ran off into the night.

The couple returned to Raton to tell their tale. Soon after, a hunting party with guns set out to find the beast. However, all they ever found were tracks leading to the final remains of the poor horse. Eventually, the men found a cave. In it was the missing Sotero, now more hairy and unkempt than ever. Sotero explained that he no longer wished to live in town and preferred the isolated lifestyle of a hermit. This is where the folktale ends and one can only guess at Sotero's ultimate fate, but clearly the townsfolk believed that he had been bitten by the Goblin Rat and turned into a werewolf as a result.

RATON FROM THE AIR.

Source:

De Aragon, Ray John. *New Mexico Book of the Undead*. The History Press, 2014.

CHAPTER 19
BURIAL GROUND BEAST

For all the skeptics and doubters of these stories, sometimes you have to admit that the coincidences within them are too much. And it's always the little things. A good example is the Crosswicks Monster of 1882, which was a theropod-type dinosaur found hiding in a hollowed-out tree, just like a similar dinosaur monster from all the way down in Oklahoma. Hoaxers and yarn spinners back then usually weren't knowledgeable or clever enough to cross-reference their stories in such a way, especially in the pre-internet age.

In this story's case, we have similar monsters being sighted in similar locations only one state away from one another. Since Illinois borders Wisconsin to the south, I found it fascinating that

Illinois had what sounded to be a werewolf sighting similar to Wisconsin's Beast of Bray Road all the way back in 1879.

BEAST OF BRAY ROAD ILLUSTRATION BY LINDA GODFREY C.1991.

Though the story of the Bray Road Beast's journey into the public consciousness begins in the late 1980s thanks to journalist Linda Godfrey, eventually Godfrey discovered that the werewolf dated back to the 1930s. Late one night in 1936, night watchman Mark Shackleman was on his way to work at the St. Coletta School for Exceptional Children. Walking across a field where an old Native American Burial ground was located, he spied a strange dog-like animal digging into the mounds. He could also smell rotten meat. Suddenly, the wolf-like being turned to look at him and stood up on its hind legs, making it about six feet tall. Thankfully for Shackleman, the beast ran away into the wild.

To the south of Wisconsin, in the neighboring state of Illinois, a similar werewolf-like beast was sighted on a Native American burial ground in the summer of 1879 near Rock River, Illinois. The story was published in the *New Orleans Times-Picayune* on August 3, 1879:

A Mysterious Monster.

Remarkable Midnight Gunning by Two Geneseo Hunters for a Strange Beast – Escape of the Varmint.

[Correspondence Chicago Times.]

GENESEO, Ill., July 30. — Esil Clouse, a well known merchant of this city, and a man named Hefner, from Rock Island, Ill., met with an adventure in the Rock River forest, adjacent to Penney's Slough, seven miles north of here, on last Friday night [July 25], that savors strongly of the marvelous. Everybody in this city knows Clouse. He is a sober, quiet, honest young married man.

Clouse and Hefner were fishing in Penney's Slough on Friday night, and about midnight they were startled by a series of the most hideous yells, emanating from the old Indian burying-ground, just over the edge of the precipitous bluff that rises a few rods back from the slough. Hefner said: "There is that animal again." On being asked to explain, he related that he had seen a large, strange animal in that neighborhood about a year previous. Both then seized their guns (double-barreled breech-loaders) and, leaving a young man named Lawson in charge of the camp, clambered up the bluff, and were soon in the old burying-ground.

Each had a lantern, and by the light of these soon saw an animal about the size of a large Newfoundland dog standing erect on its hind feet on one of the Indian graves. Clouse says that the beast had no hair, but seemed to be covered with large bony plates or scales. Two large white stripes ran down his back. His head was small, and surmounted by a pair of long pointed ears, which he flapped up and down with great facility. He stood and stared fiercely at the men, blinking in the lights of the lanterns. He pounded his breast vehemently and with his fore paws. Both Clouse and Hefner fired into his body with BB shot from a distance of about three rods. The effect was to knock the animal over; but he was immediately on his feet again, and howling like a demon. Clouse describes the sound of the shot as they struck the body to be

SKINWALKERS, WEREWOLVES, AND HELLHOUNDS OF NORTH AMERICA

similar to striking a hollow stump. They gave him another load each. He then took to racing frantically up and down an old hollow tree, about the center of the grave yard. While this was going on they gave him in all a dozen charges of heavy shot. Finally he ran into a hole in the tree. Determined to kill him if possible, the men ran to the camp and procured a couple of axes, with which they soon felled the hollow and rotten tree. The screams of the brute as the tree fell were absolutely horrible. He rushed from his lair and into the forest, returning several times and making at the men as if to attack them. He finally departed and was seen no more. The men visited the ground next day, but could detect no trace of blood. In the hollow of the tree they found the sleeve of a coat, a pocket and some buttons. Bear-traps and various devices are now planted about the brute's haunts, and hopes are entertained that he may be captured.

Though it's odd that the beast had what appeared to be scales rather than hair, the comparison was still made immediately to a Newfoundland dog, as opposed to any other similar-sized animal, which I find interesting. Then there's the pointed ears which sound to be canine-like. I also took note of how they described the creature as "standing erect on its hind feet," which indicates the beast wasn't taken to be bipedal or humanoid in stance. The usage of the term hind legs also brings to mind a dog rather than a primate or human. There is also the mention of "forepaws" rather than hands.

ROCK RIVER AREA, ILLINOIS.

The hollow tree is also interesting for a few reasons. If one wants to go full werewolf in regard to this story, they could surmise that the "sleeve of a coat, a pocket and some buttons" belonged to the monster in its human form. Or, it could have belonged to someone that the monster killed and drug back to its lair. I also find it interesting how many monsters use hollowed-out trees as lairs. In many myths, hollowed-out trees are also home to fairies, gnomes, and other supernatural entities.

Surprisingly, when one searches out the mythical animals and monsters of the Rock River region, the Winnebago Native American tribe has an oral tradition stating that when their people and the Potawatomi camped along the river banks, they encountered a terrible water demon. They said that it had horns on its head, a long tail, great jaws and fangs, and a snake-like body.[48] I halfway wonder if the monster's horns could correlate to the pointed ears seen by the two men in 1897, and if perhaps the scaly body lines up with the description of the Native American monster having the body of a snake? Of course, it's by no means a dead-ringer, but it's interesting nonetheless. And, the creature was sighted at a Native American burial ground, and it would be interesting to know if that burial ground belonged to either the Winnebago or Potawatomi tribe.

POSTCARD ALLEGEDLY DEPICTING WINNEBAGO TRIBE OF WISCONSIN.

The Winnebago monster sounded quite a bit larger than the creature seen in 1879, as it was large enough to swallow a deer or a man whole. (Perhaps the 1879 beast was a juvenile? Actually, if I were to

---

[48] I suppose this monster could be some type of variation of the Piasa Bird of Illinois, but the Piasa Bird had wings, and accounts of the Rock River demon didn't.

peg this story on anything, it would be John Keel's ultraterrestrial theory, which claimed that these cosmic beings purposely take the form of area myths. And, the Winnebago peoples did make offerings to this monster, which I also find interesting. For the sake of argument, let's say the monster was indeed a sinister ultraterrestrial. If that were the case, then why wouldn't it take the form of a local legend?

Or, perhaps there is no relation at all to the cryptid sighted in 1879 and the demon said to inhabit the depths of Rock River. Even though the 1879 cryptid certainly wasn't a traditional werewolf, maybe it was some kind of offshoot related to the one seen haunting the burial mounds of Bray Road years later? In any case, it's interesting that we have two accounts, relatively close to one another involving a werewolf-like animal associated with a Native American burial ground.

CHAPTER 20
CASE OF THE WERE-ONZA

If I was to tell you that famous Texas folklorist J. Frank Dobie killed a skinwalker, would you believe it? Furthermore, what if said skinwalker took on the form of a cryptid known as the Onza, a mystery cat similar to a puma that has been reported as far back as the days of the Conquistadors. Nah, I wouldn't believe it either. However, as with any tall tale, there might be a kernel of truth in it somewhere, so it bears repeating.

We'll start with J. Frank Dobie (1888-1964), easily my favorite folklorist. In his lifetime, he authored numerous books and articles on folklore and nature, with an emphasis on lost treasure and animal tales. As odd as this sounds, a story has circulated that Dobie killed an Onza once while down in Mexico.

J. FRANK DOBIE.

In the late 1920s, Dobie was on the hunt with C.B. Ruggles, who shared Dobie's passion for finding lost mines. Their goal was the so-called Mine of Lost Souls in the Sierras. Their encounter with the Onza began one night around the campfire when the two men heard a strange cry in the distance that they took to be a calf coming of age into a bull.

The next morning, a Mexican friend stopped by their camp to tell them that what they heard wasn't a bovine, but a large feline. Dobie and Ruggles argued with their friend, who still insisted that it was a tiger. Ruggles decided to set his two dogs off in the direction of the creature. One of the dogs, an experienced hunter named Bluntzer, took off swiftly, while the other, an Airedale, was too afraid to go in that direction. The Aerdaile had the right idea, as Bluntzer was never seen again. Dobie and Ruggles then found tracks that confirmed that their Mexican friend, whom they had doubted, was right after all. In the dirt, they found huge saucer-sized footprints of a big cat, made all the stranger by the fact that each foot was missing its outside toe.

Dobie asked their Mexican friend (who goes unnamed throughout the story) if he knew what the creature was. What Dobie writes next is worth reprinting in full as it gives tantalizing mention of a few other folkloric cryptids that he neglected to detail any further:

> The *Mestizo* said nothing. Whether he had ever heard of the onza, I do not know. He was perfectly familiar with an animal that shoots fire out of its eyes at night to make turkeys fall out of their roost.
>
> "Do you suppose," I ventured, "it could be the monster cat that the Pimas say hunts by the light of a shining stone set in its forehead?"[49]

---

[49] Dobie, *Afield with J. Frank Dobie*, p.177.

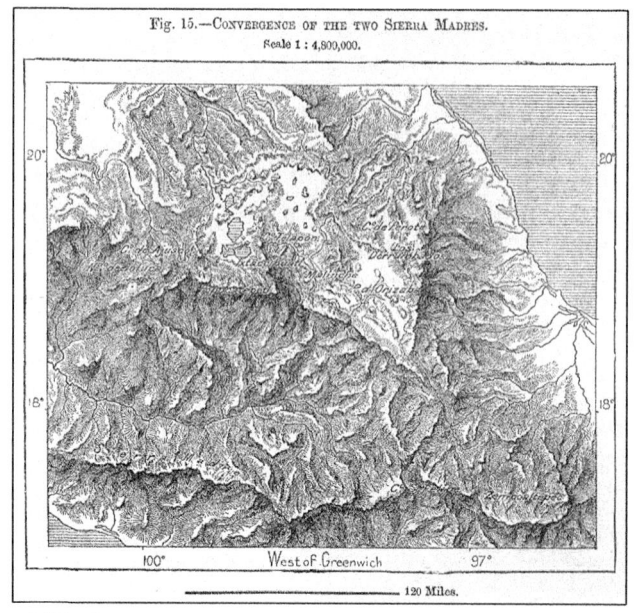

VINTAGE MAP OF THE SIERRA MADRES.

Dobie was joking, trying to chide his friends, but like you, I would love to know more about the strange animals he mentioned in passing! To make matters worse, Ruggles responded, "You'll be suggesting next that it's the track of the monster snake that strayed from the Rio Mayo."[50] (That's another cryptid I'd like to know more about!) But, I've let this meander long enough, back to the object of their quest: the Onza.

While still inspecting the tracks, they heard Bluntzer cry out a few times and then go silent. That was the last they saw of him as he never

---

[50] Ibid, p.178.

returned. Ruggles, Dobie, and the Airedale moved on without their mestizo friend until they arrived at the area of the Rio Maicoba five days later. One night at camp, the two men woke from their sleep at the sound of a strange noise. Ruggles then caught sight of a form sauntering off in the distance and called for his Airedale to chase after it. When it didn't respond, the two men realized that not only was the dog gone, but the form they saw in the distance was likely carrying it away!

The men knew there was no catching the beast in the dark and so went back to bed to resume their hunt in the morning. The next day, they found the same four-toed tracks and followed them to a mountain. There they found the poor dead Airedale, partially buried and hidden within the brush so that the animal could finish eating it later. Dobie and Ruggles set traps for the animal and caught it just as they had hoped. Dobie was shocked at the sight of the massive feline, writing, "The animal was caught in two traps. I do not believe that one alone could have held. It. Its breast was enormous, its flanks lithe."[51]

Dobie also noted that the animal was older, with some grey fur, and that it was also a female. The men shot and killed the monstrous feline, which was neither lion, tiger, panther, nor puma. It was unlike anything they had ever seen before. While carrying the carcass downhill, they ran across a group of Pima Indians who were so frightened by the sight of the carcass that they ran away. Dobie

---

[51] Ibid, p.180.

and Ruggles only heard them identify it as the Onza, the first inclination as to the beast's identity.

From around the same corner eventually came hobbling a much older Pima man, who also voiced his shock at seeing the Onza. With an old stick, he began to poke and prod at it, taking special notice of its feet. The two men asked him to explain better just what the Onza was, and he replied that the Onza was "the worst animal in the world."[52]

"Sometimes – sometimes I say – it is a cross between a bull tiger and a she lion."[53] Ruggles caught on to the "sometimes" remark and asked the old man what he meant by it. And this is where the story gets really interesting.

The old man told the men that they had done a holy deed in killing the beast, as it once terrorized his village on the Arroyo de Penasco. In his village lived a man named Ignazio, who had a wife and three sons aged ten, eight, and six. One morning, the oldest son disappeared without a trace from his own room, which was shared with the other two boys. At first, everyone thought he left early to do his chores, but by sundown, the boy was still missing.

In the same village also lived an old witch who was hideous to look at and as strong as an ox. The villagers thought that perhaps she either knew where the boy was or had possibly taken him herself. When questioned, the witch acted as though she was disparaged by the young boy's

---

[52] Ibid, p.181.
[53] Ibid.

disappearance, claiming him to be a friend. The villagers, six in all, then held her down and tortured her trying to get her to give up the boy's location, but she swore she did not know where he was even when they jammed a red-hot wire through her ear.

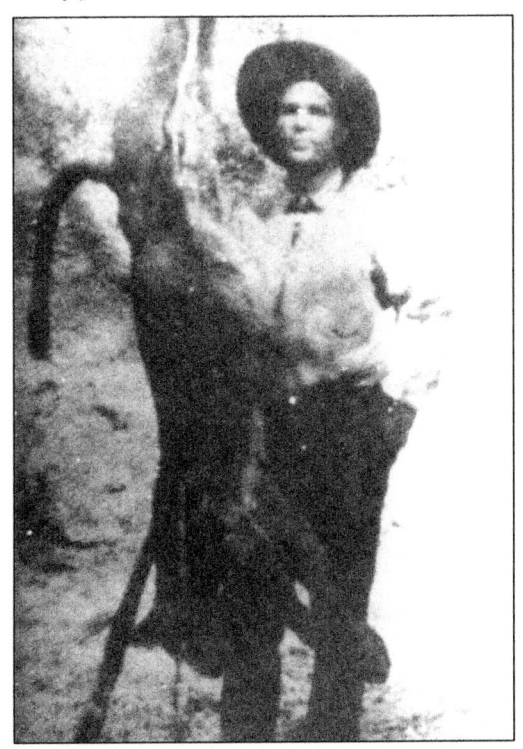

C.B. RUGGLES WITH ONZA.

That night, Igancio's next oldest son disappeared without a trace, just as the first. As such, the next night, some of the men of the village, which included the old man telling the tale, hid out near the witch's home. They had hoped she might leave, and they could follow her to a hidden lair where the boys were held. To their astonishment, they watched as the witch vanished before their eyes right as she stepped outside. Though they could see nothing, they could hear and sense a presence of some kind flying over their heads which terrified them. A bit later, the witch again materialized in front of her home and then went back inside.

The next morning, the men returned to question the witch again. This time, they upped their torture methods by sawing off her little toe on each foot with the ridges of a tough agave cactus! They also sawed off the pinky finger on both hands, and still the witch claimed she had nothing to do with the boys' disappearance.

So, that night, they set a trap for the witch in the boys' room, using the youngest son as bait. When the witch entered, this time they would lock her in so that there was no escape. Though they didn't see the witch enter, they heard the strange flying noises from the night before. When they heard a commotion from within the room, they barred the door shut so that there was no escape. But, foolishly, the men left the witch alone in the room with the poor boy. As it turned out, the men were too afraid to confront the witch at night, when her powers were strongest, and would wait until morning to face her.

When the men opened the door at first light, weapons bared, a massive Onza sprang from the room knocking over several men before darting away. The little boy was nowhere to be found, so presumably the Onza ate him. From that day

SKINWALKERS, WEREWOLVES, AND HELLHOUNDS OF NORTH AMERICA

forward, neither the witch nor the Onza was seen again.

Ruggles, clearly not drawing the connection between the witch and the Onza, said to the man, "You must have felt pretty bad for torturing any human being so much when it turned out that an onza was to blame."[54]

The old man then pointed out to the men that the Onza they carried was missing all of its outer toes, just like the witch, and that it also had holes in the ear flaps. "What more proof do you wish?" the old man asked, before telling the men that he had to be getting along.

Unfortunately, that's where Dobie leaves us with his story and doesn't fill us in or not as to whether he believed the story. But consequently, we shouldn't believe Dobie. As it turns out, while Ruggles did indeed shoot an Onza, he never did so in the company of J. Frank Dobie. This story was a pastiche on Dobie's part, which combined Ruggles' true killing of the Onza (see the photograph on page 161) with a folktale that Dobie fancied.

The old man, too, was part of the original Ruggles story. In the original version, sans Dobie, a party of Indians passed through Ruggles' camp to gawk at the Onza. They were soon followed by an old-timer, the inspiration for the character in Dobie's story. The old man told Ruggles many things about the Onza, but none of them were supernatural, and he certainly didn't relate the folktale.

---

[54] Ibid, p.186.

According to Robert E. Marshall in *The Onza*, the were-onza folktale is very common in the Sierra region of Mexico. The fact that Dobie was friends with Ruggles has never been disputed. But Ruggles has never, ever mentioned having Dobie along with him on his Onza hunt. What we do know is that in hearing the tale from Ruggles firsthand, it seems that Dobie couldn't resist injecting himself into it and then using the old man to tell the oft-repeated were-onza folktale at the end.

After all, one of Dobie's better-known books was titled *I'll Tell You a Tale...*

Sources:

Dobie, J. Frank. *Afield With J. Frank Dobie: Tales of Critters, Campfires, and the Hunting Trail.* High Lonesome Books, 1992.

Marshall, Robert E. *The Onza: The Story of the Search for the Mysterious Cat of the Mexican Highlands.* Exposition Press, 1961

CHAPTER 21

WHAT WAS THE WAHHOO?

Late 1870s Nevada was the location of a flap of sightings of a cryptid dubbed alternatively as the Wahhoo and the Whoahaw. The beast was similar in size and description to the Shunka Warak'in. Some cryptozoologists (notably David Weatherly) think it may have even been of the same species. As such, the Whoahaw/Wahhoo might well be another Borophagus, a hyena-like dog from the Pleistocene epoch. Or, if not that, perhaps another supernatural were-creature...

The animal was first reported in Nevada in the *Reno Gazette-Journal* on August 26, 1879, on page three:

THE WHOAHAW.

—

A Hunting Party's Experience — The Strange Creature that Dominates Deeth — Stories of His Ferocity— Abundance of Game and Good Sport.

Richard Smith, the express agent, and his brother H. R., got back last Sunday night from their hunting expedition. They shot over the country around about Deeth and Halleck. Game was abundant. During the trip they bagged 125 prairie chickens and one lynx, besides untold numbers of sage hens, rabbits, ducks, etc. The singular number of lynx shot by the party would appear to indicate a scarcity of large game in that section of the state explored by the expedition. One might suppose that where birds were so abundant, lynx and other of their four footed enemies would be more numerous. It is a striking fact that they killed only one of the carnivora during the trip. But there is an explanation for the scarcity of such animals that will be strange to many readers. The whole region round about Deeth is dominated by

A MYSTERIOUS BEAST known locally as the Whoahaw, an animal supposed to be a cross between the grizzly bear and the coyote. As the mule combines all the bad qualities of the horse and the ass, so does this hybrid display the courage and ferocity of the grizzly joined to the cunning and treachery of the coyote. The whoahaw has never been seen by daylight. He roams and ravages only at night. The beast has been known to carry off a horse. Cattle and sheep are often borne away by the monster. Mules he never attacks, for some unexplained reason. The brothers often sat up far into the night listening to the ranchmen's tales of the strength and ferocity of the whoahaw. There is supposed to be only one of them in that section of the country, he has never been distinctly seen, but some of the ranchers have caught glimpses of him prowling about in the darkness. They always had business of importance to attend to somewhere else upon such occasions. The recital of tales about the fearful creature one night,

CURDLED THE BLOOD of H. R. Smith almost to coagulation. Richard says the ranchmen's stories often ran his own circulation down from seventy to forty beats a minute. Nothing but the speedy administration of tea or other stimulant could have enabled them to pull through those narratives. The brothers camped in the vicinity several nights, almost daring to hope that they might catch a glimpse of the dangerous hybrid. But they saw nothing of him, although one midnight they heard far off an echoing sound like "whoa-----haw," which the ranchmen said was the cry of the monster, and from which they gave him his name. Should some adventurous hunter eventually cope with and kill the curious beast it is to be hoped for the sake of science, that, his bones and skin will be carefully preserved. The brothers did not meet with any exciting adventures during their trip. They were much impressed with exceeding swiftness of the coyote, when stimulated to exertion by the presence of fine shot under the skin. In order to observe his velocity they frequently introduced fine shot under the hide of strugglin' coyotes, always with the most gratifying results. They recommend the neighborhood of Deeth for hunting, but "Beware," they say, "of the whoahaw."

On August 29th, the monster was sighted again outside a home in Reno. This time it displayed supernatural qualities such as fiery, glowing eyes and was called the Wahhoo in the article printed in the *Reno Gazette-Journal* on September 4, 1879:

Was It A Wahhoo?

A. A. Adams is a well-known and highly respected German citizen. His residence is near the corner of Fourth and Chestnut streets. Mr. Adams is a bachelor, and lives in a small cottage [in Reno]. He is not superstitious, and never clouds his mind with ardent spirits. ... So when he heard some heavy animal walking slowly up and down his verandah last Friday night [August 29], he did not suppose that the noises were in any way supernatural. He simply wondered what kind of a beast could have got into his yard. He listened, and could distinctly hear the tread of some four-footed creature, as it slowly trod to and fro. He could even hear the scratch of the creature's claws on the boards. His curiosity at length aroused, Mr. Adams determined to take a look at the pedestrian on his portico.

He rose from his bed, and, putting on an additional garment, he stepped forth into the rheumy and unpurged air of midnight. The moon was shining from a cloudless sky, and by its sight seemed a large black bulldog. The animal stopped in its walk, and turned two brilliant, fiery eyes upon Mr. Adams. They glowed with an unnatural brightness; looking more like hot coals than visual organs. He noticed, too, that its 'snoot' was very long, like a pig's; and its tail of surprising length, stuck straight out behind. Mr. Adams clearly saw that, whatever his strange visitor might be, it was no bulldog. After looking at him steadily for over a minute, the beast slowly retreated to the fence, which it climbed by means of its claws, after the manner of a cat. Perched upon the top of the fence, the creature sat, and resumed its survey of the astonished German. Mr. Adams thought he would direct a stream of water from the garden hose upon the animal, and thereby induce it to retire. He did so, but, to his amazement, the creature remained immovable, merely presenting its snout to the stream, its body enveloped in a cloud of spray. Mr. Adams persevered in the hydropathic treatment for about ten minutes, but still the beast kept its position, its eyes glaring at him like the red lights of a railway train.

Mr. Adams owns to a feeling of dread at the creature's peculiar persistence under the circumstances, and began to think that ghost stories might be true after all. He retreated into the house and locked the door. He looked out of the window, and there still sat the animal on the top of the fence, its baleful eyes throwing a lurid glare into the room. Mr. Adams now felt a great fall in the temperature. He was shivering with cold. He thought he would fire a charge of shot at the brute, and got out his gun for the purpose. He loaded the weapon hastily, but after he had put on the caps, concluded he wouldn't fire after all. He pulled down the blinds, and went back to bed.

He listened for a long time, but heard no more footsteps. The cold continued, and Mr. Adams shivered nearly all night, and got very little rest in consequence. At daylight next morning he was out, and made a careful search of the yard, closely examined the fence and porch, but discovered no trace of the strange beast. He put his gun in careful order, and made up his mind that should the creature come again he would fire upon it at sight. He was surprised to find, on cleaning the weapon, that in loading it the night before, he had put the shot in first, and the powder afterward....

Mr. Adams carefully loaded the gun that day, putting in the powder first to avoid the mistakes apt to attend that operation when performed in the dark. The following night he sat up late in company, with a countryman of his, but saw nothing unusual, nor has he since been visited by the mysterious beast. No animal answering to the description is known to exist in this section of the country.

In addition to the peculiarities already described, Mr. Adams said it had a long, slender neck. Could it have been one of those ferocious hybrids called wahhoos, which are said to prowl at night in the neighborhood of Halleck and Deeth?... The mystery may yet be cleared up, but now the question is, among many who hear the story, was it a wahhoo?"

Stories of the animal continued to pour in, such as this one on September 9, 1879, from the *Reno Evening Gazette*:

Wahhoo, or What?

A strange looking animal was seen by two sportsmen on the road about two miles from Peavine last Sunday. This creature was not unlike a coyote but larger, yet too small for a bear. It was running on the side of a hill with wonderful speed, and disappeared in a moment. Could the beast have been a Wahhoo?"

And then, only three days later in the same paper, this story appeared, which gave it another

European werewolf trait, that being exhuming graves to consume the corpses!

The Wild Wahhoo!
A "Man-Eater" that opens the Graves of the Dead. A Full Description of the Strange Beast—Its Pedal Peculiarities—Its Haunts in the Hills—Found in Nevada, Idaho and Montana—A Creature with the Form of a Dog and the Voice of a Jackass.

A recent number of the Gazette contained some account of an animal found in the neighborhood of Halleck and Deeth, Nevada, known in that section of country as the "Wahhoo." It appears that the creature is not known to naturalists and finds no place in the catalogs of writers upon zoology. Some readers of the article referred to for this reason supposed the whole story to be a hoax. But it must be remembered that every day the researches of scientists are bringing to light hitherto unknown animals and plants, in every quarter of the globe. Animals well-known locally, in some remote localities of the earth, often prove entirely new and strange to the world of science. The narratives of travelers are often received with a great deal of incredulity because they frequently contain descriptions of things before unheard of. When Du Chaillu discovered the gorilla in Africa, scientists were slow to believe in the existence of the animal. Nearer home there is a fish in Idaho called the "redfish," which is familiar to the people of that territory, yet has never been scientifically described, and of which no specimen has yet been placed in the Smithsonian Institute.

The account of the Wahhoo which follows is plain and unvarnished, and it may yet be found that this strange beast will possess a high scientific interest to workers in the field of natural history. In the brief and imperfect description of the Wahhoo to which reference has already been made, were given some data relating to the animal, which were furnished by Richard Smith, the agent of Wells, Fargo & Co.'s express, at Reno.

That gentleman, while hunting in the neighborhood of Halleck, heard from residents of that locality many stories of the Wahhoo and its peculiarities. He did not succeed in catching a glimpse of one, but his brother who was with him succeeded in obtaining the dressed hide of a Wahhoo and took it with him to Los Angeles on his return from the expedition. Mr. Smith's Reno friends, to whom he repeated some of the stories he had heard of the strange creature, were skeptical of their truth. But the publication of the article in the Gazette brought to light some additional testimony concerning the curious beast. Before proceeding with an entirely new evidence, it will be well to state what the people about Deeth say of the animal. It is they who are known both as the Wahhoo and the maneater.

The former appellation is supposed to have been given it in imitation of the peculiar noise it makes. The latter designation originated in the known propensity of the beast to dig up and devour bodies of the dead. Wahhoos which have been killed near Deeth exhibit a peculiar structure. The legs are short, and the paws very large proportionally, furnished with strong projecting claws of great length. This formation enables the creature to dig with ease and rapidity. The body is long and slender, the tail of medium length and usually curved over the back, the neck short, the head broad, and the jaws provided with formidable teeth. The skin is covered with long, fine hair. Its prevailing color is black, spotted with white. In weight it varies from fifty to seventy-five pounds. The creature is larger than a coyote, and in appearance, when seen at a distance, not unlike a large dog. In conversation with Mr. Smith, a young man said that he had shot a number of Wahhoos, that he carefully measured each specimen, and found that the left legs of each were somewhat shorter than the right legs. Although his informant persisted in the assertion, a statement must be regarded with great caution.

The probability is that he measured a malformed specimen and jumped to the conclusion that the others showed the same peculiarities. The young man stated, as an explanation for the inequality in the length of the creature's legs, that the Wahhoo was found only upon the hills, along the sides of which it was constantly traveling. The unequal length of its legs would be advantageous to the animal in traversing the hillsides. It would indeed be strange if nature had provided such a marvelous adaptation of structure to fit the creature for ranging upon the sides of hills. Incredible as such a statement certainly is, it might possibly be true. Knowing in what strange forms of life have inhabited the earth in bygone epochs, nothing seems impossible in animated nature. In the presence of the fossil remains of the Eohippus, or fivetoed horse, a laterally unequal wahhoo would not seem so strange a creature after all.

Daniel Roberts, an express messenger on the Central Pacific Railroad, states that in Montana wahhoos are not uncommon. He saw and heard the creature in Idaho in 1867. He has vivid recollection of his first sight of one of the beasts. He was approaching a station in Beaver canyon, one evening in the summer of that year, after a long journey on horseback. On the way up the canyon he heard what he supposed was the bray of a mule. He remarked to his companion, who was familiar with the country, that they must be near the camp. He was told that the noise was made by a wahhoo, and shortly afterward they saw the animal sitting on its haunches above them and giving utterance to the dismal cry, which had deceived Mr. Roberts. The creature walked along the edge of the precipice for some distance, at intervals sitting upon its haunches and sending forth its prolonged, wailing bay.

A man named Thomas, well-known to Mr. Roberts, shortly after killed a wahhoo on the Montana road, near the Camas Creek station. It weighed about seventy pounds and fought wickedly after being wounded, until it was finally dispatched. Not long after that, Mr. Roberts, in company with Mr. Bassett, a superintendent in the employ of the Western Union telegraph company, saw two wahhoos together near a place called Summit Station. He states that the animal is well-known all over Montana. It is very shy, nocturnal in its habits, and abides in the wilderness away from the habitations of men. It is going to these reasons that so little is yet known of the wahhoo. The foregoing meager description is all that the Gazette has been able to learn of the mysterious beast. It is published in the hope that the attention of some zoologist may be drawn to the fact of the existence of such a creature, and that the animal may prove a subject for the study and investigation of someone qualified to classify and describe it. All communications designed to throw any light upon the nature and habits of the wahhoo will be gratefully acknowledged.

This was, in my opinion, the last legitimate article on the Wahhoo, as the next two I found were satiric in nature. I attribute this partly to the odd belief that the animal was lopsided, with longer legs on the right side (I think the paper's speculation that Smith measured a malformed specimen was more likely). This odd trait would humorously be attributed to the animals in the last article to cover them at the time.

Our next sighting was reported five days after the previous article in the *Weekly Reno Gazette* published on September the 18th (though the letter was written on the 17th):

A Wahhoo Seen Near Wadsworth — A Party in Pursuit.

Ed. Gazette:—Report was brought to town yesterday that a wahhoo had been seen in the mountains west of town. The night before, the people of Jones' ranch had been aroused by the wahhoo's long-drawn howl, which was likened to a shrill fog-whistle. They saw the mountains illumined as with an electric light.

This they found was owing to the glare of the creature's eyeballs. It sat upon a neighboring cliff, and so brilliant was the light emitted that none could gaze upon the creature, even for an instant.

This report, backed by authority, so excited our nimrods that a hunt was organized immediately. Jake Lewis, J. W. Holbrook, Wm. Pierson and others started this morning, and brilliant work is looked for before the close of day.

Anticipating that a lengthened hunt might prove necessary, the party laid in provisions, of which the following is a summary: Whiskey, 200 rounds ammunition, demijohn, 1 piece bacon, limes, 1 bottle whiskey, 1 box cigars, 50 rounds additional whiskey, more whiskey.

The result of the chase is awaited with breathless anxiety. A special reporter accompanied the party, and full particulars will be given on their return.

PREHISTORIC BOROPHAGUS.

As you can tell from the supplies that included whiskey and more whiskey, this article was poking fun at the sighting, if it even happened. The likelihood that the animal's eyes were bright enough to cause a person to look away was also unlikely and seemed to be a spoof of earlier articles that described the animal's eyes. I could find no more reports on the animal from 1879. The next article was published in the *Reno Evening Gazette* on January 8, 1880. As it turned out, it would tell of the Wahhoo pack's final stand...

Totally Extinct
Waylaying the Wahoo on a Mountain Side
The Last of These Strange Animals.

The cold weather is said to have killed off all the wahoos about Halleck and Deeth. A Wells-Fargo messenger reports that on last Saturday morning a party of Deeth hunters found wahoo tracks in the snow five miles northeast of the station. The severity of the weather appeared to have forced the animals to band together, as the tracks could not have been made by less than six different animals.

The circumstance excited the interest of the hunters, for anyone who knows what a wahoo is, knows full well that the creature is one of the most unsocial of all animated beings. The hunters determined to follow up the broad trail made by the wahoos, and at once started in pursuit. The tracks led them around the base of a high mountain and constantly ascended in a continuous spiral. The hunters followed the trail for hours, constantly climbing higher and higher, until at length the summit was reached, and the trail began to wind back down the mountain.

The hunters were now thoroughly exasperated and pressed on with fierce determination. The chase went on for hours until they reached the plain again and found that the wahoo's track had some proposed to give up the pursuit, but one of the party said if they would follow him they would fix the wahoos. He reminded them that owing to the fact that the wahoos' left legs are shorter than its right, the creature always walks on the hillside from right to left. His proposal was that that hunters should ascend the hill in the opposite way, and thus head off the wahoos and take them at a disadvantage.

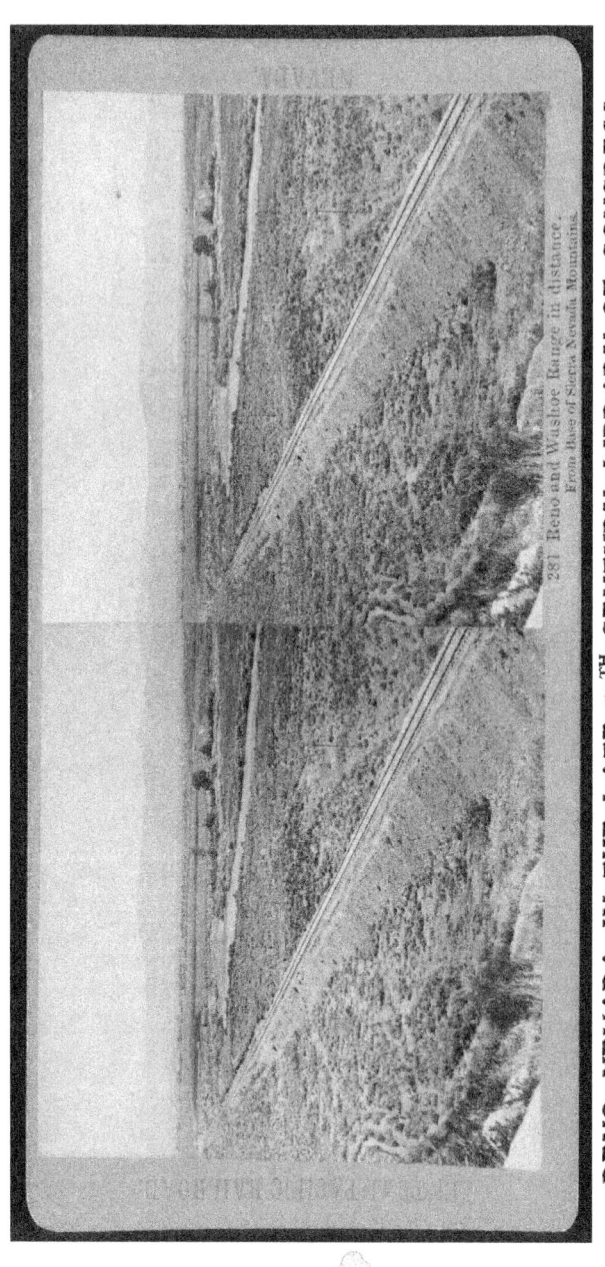

RENO, NEVADA, IN THE LATE 19TH CENTURY. LIBRARY OF CONGRESS.

SKINWALKERS, WEREWOLVES, AND HELLHOUNDS OF NORTH AMERICA

So with fresh enthusiasm the party started off again, and after an hours' climb they met six wahoos face to face, halfway up the summit. Three of the creatures fell at the first fire. The others tried to turn and run but owing to their legs being shorter on one side than on the other they immediately lost their balance and rolled helplessly to the bottom of the slope, where the hunters subsequently found their lifeless carcasses.

This little band of devoted wahoos probably was the last of these curious animals. The few others that roamed the hills in the vicinity of Deeth and Halleck are believed to have perished in the late cold snap, and thus the wahoo, like the dodo, may at last be considered extinct.

Again, I find this story somewhat troubling because I feel it is folkloric more than anything else. The detail about the right and left legs, as I stated earlier, is carried over into this story from a previous article. However, we shall not let the last two articles destroy the credibility of the Wahhoo.

The Wahhoo's saving grace may well be the previous article published on September 12, 1879, in the *Reno Evening Gazette*. That article told how the Wahhoo had also been seen in Idaho and Montana, which lines up with what we learned in a previous chapter. As you'll no doubt remember, Israel Hutchins shot one of the creatures in Montana, though this was never reported in the local papers that I know of. That this article recounts additional sightings in Montana bolsters not only the Ringdocus sightings, in which a body was preserved, but also the Wahhoo sightings. After all, since we have concrete proof that the Ringdocus/Shunka Warak'in was real, why then couldn't the Wahhoo have existed as well?

> # THE WILD WAHHOO!
>
> ## A "Man-Eater" that Opens the Graves of the Dead.
>
> A Full Description of the Strange Beast— its Pedal Peculiarities — Its Haunts in the Hills —Found in Nevada, Idaho and Montana—A Creature with the Form of a Dog and the Voice of a Jackass.

RENO EVENING GAZETTE 9-12-79.

Sources:

Weatherly, David. *Silver State Monsters: Cryptids and Legends of Arizona.* Nevada: Leprechaun Press, 2019.

SKINWALKERS, WEREWOLVES, AND HELLHOUNDS OF NORTH AMERICA

THE MONSTER WAS A GHOUL

The following story appeared in the *Athens Banner Watchman* on February 19, 1884:

FEEDING UPON GRAVES.

The strange animal which has been desecrating graves in Perry Township, Wood county, [Ohio] has again been seen. A gentleman whose veracity is not questioned gives this description of the novel grave-yard ghoul: Its neck and breast are white and the rest of the body is black; the tracks of its front feet are about eight inches long and three wide, making impressions in the snow with its claws about twice the length of a man's finger. The tracks made by the hind feet are nearly round, and about the size of a large dog's, except the claws, which are longer and sharper. The animal is about, three feet long and eighteen inches high.

It burrows into the ground in the grave yard, and penetrating the coffins therein contained; devours the contents thereof. It travels with such rapidity that all attempts thus far to kill it have been futile. The man who last saw the animal says it was in the middle of the road, having gone from a farm by literally tearing the fence to pieces. His dog gave chase to the animal, but soon returned scared almost to death.

The people living, in the vicinity having frequently heard loud noise which are supposed to have emanated from this peculiar unnamed, unknown beast. The animal is said to be slowly working its way to Toledo.

This animal sounds a bit like the Wahhoo covered in the previous chapter, as it, too, dug up graves to get at the corpses, so perhaps it was? Furthermore, an old tradition from medieval Europe stated that the werewolf had a habit of devouring recently buried corpses.

CHAPTER 22
RETURN OF THE DOG EATER

Of all the states in the U.S., Georgia has an odd selection of werewolf stories, one of which was covered earlier. The story we're about to examine was printed in the July 6, 1896, *Atlanta Constitution* and concerned a little community called Comer. Though at a brisk reading it may appear that this is a run-of-the-mill "strange animal" account rather than a potential werewolf story, the devil is in the details. In this case, a small humanoid footprint implies a tie to lycanthropy within the account. However, see if you can spot a suspicious witness name that somewhat tarnishes the article:

COWBOYS & DOGMEN

A STRANGE ANIMAL
That Is Creating Terror Near the Town of Comer.

Comer, Ga., July 5.—(Special.)—A report reaches here from Five Forks that a very frightful and ferocious beast was seen by some children in a field near that place last Tuesday evening, and that their dog has not been seen since a combat with it. Late in the evening it was seen again and heard in a low undertone howl near Harry Foot's house. Wilt Gholston, a colored man living at Five Forks, claims that there was something very unusual in a swamp near Harry Foot's house as he passed there about dark Tuesday night. Its track is very much like that of a baby foot, except there is an imprint of sharp toes.

In a path near that place has been found the blood, horns and a few bones of a goat. As there are no goats near that place it is supposed that this animal brought its food from a pasture near Mr. Jim Faulkner's, where was seen the morning before, and where several pigs have been destroyed.

A crowd of men were on the hunt with guns, lights and dogs Tuesday night late, but the dogs would not do more than track to the edge of a big swamp wherein it is supposed this animal at the time was stopping.

A cow which has lately been running in this swamp came home not many days ago with the flesh on her shoulders, one of her ears and

SKINWALKERS, WEREWOLVES AND HELL HOUNDS OF NORTH AMERICA

flanks badly torn, having lost a great deal of blood.

David Weatherly, who gave me this story, pointed out in his *Peach State Monsters* that the name Harry Foot seems suspicious. (As in "hairy foot" since a footprint of a werewolf plays into the story.) However, that name is this story's first and only real strike to its credibility.

COMER, GEORGIA, POSTCARD.

It's a bit of a stretch, but 140 miles to the south of Comer, somewhere in Laurens County, in 1882, a monster was reported to be roaming the swamps below farmland belonging to Rufus T. Beacham. The blurb, as printed in the *Atlanta Constitution* on August 18, 1882, read:

A Supernatural monster has been seen more than once in the swamp below Mr. Rufus T.

Beacham's. Dogs and guns have so far proved useless in trying to bring him in.

Could it be that I'm simply grasping at straws, or was this possibly the same beast? We will likely never know. Nor were there any follow-up articles on the Comer Creature that we know of. The only thing tangent to them came about 25 years later when in 1923, the *Atlanta Constitution* reported on some random animal mutilations blamed on a large wolf in the small mountain community of Chipley. The June 14, 1923 *Constitution* reported on the beast's tracks:

> The tracks of the beast are somewhat similar to those of a dog but much larger. Those that have been favored with a view of the monster declare that it is much larger than a dog and travels with an entirely different gait.

Of course, back in those days, random, strange predatory animals showing up and disappearing wasn't uncommon. One of the only ones to stick around and get a true "flap" of sightings was the "Dog Eater" of Kentucky, only one state away from Georgia to the north of Tennessee. As covered in a previous chapter, for a span of six years starting in 1885, the Dog Eater terrorized Kentucky by killing dogs as the name implied. Could the Dog Eater have migrated south to Georgia? Records actually show that the canine-beast did migrate to Tennessee by the year 1892, so perhaps by 1897 it was in Georgia?

SKINWALKERS, WEREWOLVES AND HELL HOUNDS OF NORTH AMERICA

The similarities are certainly there, including the footprints. An article on the Kentucky Dog Eater from 1891 described the footprints as heavily clawed and being more like those of a bird's rather than a dog's. The article stated, "The tracks left by the animal are similar to those made by a bird, though of course magnified many times, and showing that it has powerful talons." Since a paw print is circular, and a bird's webbed foot is more elongated, I think a comparison could be drawn to the footprint compared to a baby's foot with claws in the 1896 account out of Comer. Furthermore, in the 1923 incident, it was reported that it was mostly dogs that were killed by the beast, which was shot one night by hunters before it disappeared, never to be seen again. Be it a bonafide werewolf or an offshoot of Kentucky's "Dog Eater," the mystery lingers.

WEREWOLF OF THE BIG APPLE

The Trenton Evening Times reported the following on October 21, 1897:

A NEW YORK WEREWOLF.

Strange Delusion of a Man Who Crawls on All Fours

NEW YORK, Oct 21 James Rubinstein thinks he is a werewolf. He walks on all fours and howls like a wolf. A werewolf was in legendary lore supposed to be a human who, having given offense to some supernatural being, was metamorphosed by the latter into the shape of a wolf. The soul, however, retained all its human attributes, passions and desires. Rubinstein came to this country several years ago from Germany. A week ago he began showing signs of the approach of his mysterious sickness. His wife noticed that he would frequently drop on all fours and crawl around as if in search of something. Yesterday Rubinstein crawled up to his wife and barked fiercely. Then he snarled and snapped at her, and when she fled from the room he howled like a lost soul. The frightened woman sent for an ambulance and had her husband taken to the hospital.

POSTSCRIPT
THE ORIGINS OF SKINWALKER RANCH

It's become a bit of tradition to end each of these books with a special chapter or postscript detailing a fantastic location. In the last two volumes we covered a vampire's haunted grave in Texas and an Egyptian city in the Grand Canyon. For this volume, we shall turn our attention to the haunted Skinwalker Ranch. And, of all the haunted spots in America, none of them can compare to the notorious Utah ranch. Though the name suggests a connection solely to werewolves, in actuality, it runs the full gamut of UFO, cryptid, and werewolf sightings!

COWBOYS & DOGMEN

Stories of the strange ranch rose to prominence in the mid-1990s when the new owners began seeing disturbing things on the property. UFOs, glowing orbs of light, and portals could be seen in the skies regularly. Cattle were often found mutilated with surgical precision, much in the style of the late 1970s cattle mutilation flap. But, most important to the ranch's namesake, they also saw gigantic wolves said to be four times larger than a normal wolf in addition to traditional skinwalker-like creatures.

**DUSCHESNE COUNTY, UTAH
BY JOHN VACHON APRIL 1942.
(LIBRARY OF CONGRESS)**

To the uninitiated, this might seem like too much. After all, UFOs don't mix it up with werewolves, do they? Not traditionally they don't, and not in most European folklore. But there are certain places on Earth that experts have dubbed

SKINWALKERS, WEREWOLVES AND HELL HOUNDS OF NORTH AMERICA

"window areas," which are hotspots not only for UFOs and ghosts, but also for mystery creatures. UFOs have even been seen over Loch Ness in Scotland, for instance, though most people don't know this. Researchers like Jacques Vallée (*Passport to Magonia: From Folklore to Flying Saucers*) and John Keel (*The Mothman Prophecies*) were among the first to connect the dots that most all things that "go bump in the night" seem to be related in some way. Keel took note of the fact that in addition to the cryptid-like Mothman, UFOs, ghosts, and Men in Black were sighted all over Point Pleasant, West Virginia, during the Mothman flap of the late 1960s. Similarly, Vallée was one of the first to point out the parallels between ancient fairy lore and modern UFO abduction cases.

So, the more one becomes accustomed to the unexplained, the more one realizes that all of these strange beings and creatures seem to be connected somehow, which oddly enough extends to skinwalkers and UFOs, or "sky beings" as Native Americans might call their occupants.

In 1994, what is now known as the Skinwalker Ranch, but was then known as the old Myers Ranch, was purchased by Terry and Gwen Sherman to run cattle on. As stated earlier, many of the cattle ended up dead, either from UFO-like mutilations or from attacks by mysterious, wolf-like predators. In fact, the Shermans got shed of the place by 1996 it proved so stressful on them and sold it to Robert Bigelow, owner of the National

Institute for Discovery Science (NIDS). For ten years, NIDS accumulated what Charles Fort would have called the "damned data" as they made a study of literal monsters. Since then, Skinwalker Ranch has nearly gained as much notoriety as places like Roswell, New Mexico, and the aforementioned home of Mothman, Point Pleasant, West Virginia.

But what is it that makes Skinwalker Ranch such a haunted locale? Going all the way back to the Trail of Tears, some say that the Navajo cursed a certain portion of the land in the Uinta Basin which today serves as the Ute reservation. The Ute even call this area the Path of the Skinwalker and mount animal skulls onto some of their fenceposts in hopes of warding off the witches. As for the Skinwalker Ranch property, which borders the Ute Reservation, allegedly no Ute will dare set foot on it.

But why the curse on the Utes? The Utes' history with the Navajo is a complicated one. Initially, the Utes and Navajos would occasionally align to defeat common enemies. That all changed when the Utes themselves began to subjugate the Navajos and sell them on the slave markets in New Mexico prior to the Civil War. During the Civil War, some of the Utes aligned themselves with Kit Carson in his military campaign against the Navajo. Ever since then, the Navajo have despised the Ute, which led to the Ute belief that the Navajos cursed them with a plague of skinwalkers. Specifically, the Utes seem to believe in one head skinwalker that lives in a spot not far from the ranch called Dark Canyon. Supposedly in Dark Canyon can be found ancient petroglyphs depicting said skinwalker. However, all academic requests to see the petroglyphs have been denied by the tribal government who fear the skinwalker to this day. However, all that said, the counter argument is that even the Navajo wouldn't trust skinwalkers or make any type of deal with them to begin with.

UTE TRIBE POSSIBLY IN COLORADO OR UTAH.

Though I had hoped to perhaps unearth some bonafide Wild West era Skinwalker Ranch stories, unfortunately, I wasn't able to do so myself. However, researchers Gary and Wendy Swanson have made it a mission of theirs in recent years to collect skinwalker lore from the region. Their book, *Skinwalker: Guardian of the Last Portal*, tells of some of the earlier encounters on Skinwalker Ranch back when it was owned by the Myers. A witness, 84 years old at the time of the book's publication in 2020, wrote to the Swansons to tell them how he and his cousin would sneak onto Old Man Meyers' ranch to camp. They managed to sneak past Meyers' watchful eye by taking a little raft up the river to camp within a canyon. While there, they observed a glowing ball of light float through the air, which was very similar to sightings had by the Shermans years later.

While this in of itself wasn't terribly interesting, it did lead to the boys asking their elders about the ranch. Reportedly, some of the scuttlebutt was that the "ranchers used to say that werewolves lived up [on the ridge]!"[55] One of the boys' fathers also recalled seeing the glowing orbs back in his day when he would hunt deer in the area. Furthermore, he said that the orbs would scare off the cattle. The 84-year-old man who wrote the Swansons also recalled "three different instances where cattle on three separate ranches had been found dead..."[56] The man went on to relate that there were no signs of what killed the cattle. It also wasn't limited to the Myers ranch and extended to two other ranches. "[I]t put fear into the ranchers, and it was what all the kids talked about over at the school, because it was really scary."[57] The animals had been gutted, which struck everyone as strange since a predator would have gone for the meaty parts of the cow, but not the inner organs. This was, of course, prior to

---

[55] Swanson, *Skinwalker: Guardian of the Last Portal*, p.79.
[56] Ibid.
[57] Ibid.

SKINWALKERS, WEREWOLVES AND HELL HOUNDS OF NORTH AMERICA

THE MASONIC CONNECTION?

In addition to Native American lore, the Skinwalker Ranch is also tied to Masonic mysticism in a very unexpected way. Though the Masons were mostly associated with well-to-do Anglo men back in the 19th Century, there were also African American chapters. At Fort Duchesne near the Ute reservation were a group of Masonic Buffalo soldiers as it turns out. It's possible that this Masonic Chapter carved a Masonic symbol along Skinwalker Ridge. It was carved in a precarious place, as though the carver would have to be hung upside down to do so as it's several feet below the top of the ridge. Why they carved it there is a mystery, but to this day, the Utes recall the Masonic rites practiced by the Buffalo Soldiers. They should since many modern Ute homes are built over the graveyard of the Buffalo Soldiers of Fort Duchesne and are said to be haunted. Also worth mentioning is a water filled ravine called Bottle Hollow (because the soldiers used to toss their bottle caps into it). The ravine was filled with water in 1970 and is haunted by a spectral water serpent that is said to have killed several people. Bottle Hollow runs right along the Skinwalker Ranch, and considering the ranch has UFO and werewolf sightings, why not a water monster as well?

the widespread cattle mutilations of the 1970s. Judging by the 84-year-old witness saying that they were in school at the time, the story likely took place in the 1940s. "I remember my own father and his brother, my uncle, talking about it because my uncle also lost one cow. My uncle said the cow's tail was gone as well as her ears, and something or someone had also cut off her eyelids!"[58]

The man said that after the mutilation incidents he quit camping at the Myers Place. He also heard reports of one of the Myers ranch hands shooting at some type of strange creature to no avail. Apparently, some of these deaths were blamed on the Navajo. The witness wrote, "...the rancher's association was going out in different posses after what they called the 'Skinwalker witches.' They were suddenly convinced that the Navajo tribe south of us had created this witch to run the whites and Utes out of the area."[59]

Of course, we have to entertain the notion that the teller of this tale may have read about the notorious Skinwalker Ranch and decided to make up a story about it. While technically that is a possibility, it still wouldn't surprise me at all to find out that it was true. If anything bothers me personally about the Skinwalker Ranch's credibility, it's that strangely enough, so far no one seems to have found any record from the Myers themselves alleging paranormal activity on their ranch.[60]

In fact, in a memoir, Edith Myers described the ranch as "paradise" and lived alone there for

---

[58] Ibid.
[59] Ibid, p.80.
[60] Remember, the account just given purports to tell of the Myers shooting at Skinwalkers, but it did not come from the Myers themselves, so it should still be taken with a grain of salt.

several years after the death of her husband, Kenneth. This seems odd since the Sherman family who owned the ranch were terrified to be there one at a time. Why was this? Were the Myers under some form of spiritual protection not afforded the Shermans years later? Did the Myers perhaps have supernatural incidents and encounters and simply chose not to talk about them? Or, for the most far out theory, and also my favorite, were the Myers in some way in on and complacent with the secret of what would one day be known as Skinwalker Ranch?

If the accounts of the Shermans as published in the breakthrough book, 2005's *Hunt for the Skinwalker*, are true, then the latter theory just might be right. According to the Shermans, when they acquired the ranch, they took note of the many double locks and heavy-duty latches on all the ranch doors and windows, as though the Myers had been fearful of something outside. In *Hunt for the Skinwalker*, Colm A. Kelleher and George Knapp wrote:

> When the [Shermans] first entered the small ranch house that was to be their home, they felt a chill. Every door had several large, heavy-duty dead bolts on both the inside and outside. All of the windows were bolted, and at each end of the farmhouse, large metal chains attached to huge steel rings were embedded securely into the wall. The previous owners had apparently chained very large guard dogs on both ends of

the house. And they had barred the windows and put dead bolts on both sides of each door.[61]

Furthermore, there was a strange clause in the real estate contract that stated that the former owners were to be notified of any digging on the property. This brings to mind fears of disturbing Native American burial grounds. Gwen Sherman told Ryan Skinner, author of *Digging Into Skinwalker Ranch*, the following as well,

> When Garth Myers the executor of the estate of Ken and Edith Myers sold us the Ranch, he never mentioned anything to us about what was going on there. All he did was instruct us not to dig with a backhoe or move the big rock by the middle Homestead that appeared to have rolled off the hill.[62]

So what are we to make of the werewolves that skulk across the ground while UFOs streak through the skies of Skinwalker Ranch? Although these ties between Native American curses and aliens from other worlds may seem to be strange bedfellows, one shouldn't forget that nearly all Native Americans have legends of "other worlds." However, in their context, other worlds typically meant portals into alternate dimensions and parallel realities.

---

[61] Kelleher and Knapp, *Hunt for the Skinwalker*, pp.10-11.
[62] Skinner, *Digging Into Skinwalker Ranch*, p.39.

SKINWALKERS, WEREWOLVES AND HELL HOUNDS OF NORTH AMERICA

In fact, the Shermans occasionally employed a Native American ranch hand who had these beliefs. This man wrote to the Swansons to tell that according to what he knew from his own experience and others in the area that the ranch served as a gateway to a parallel dimension. According to the man, the previous owners, presumably the Myers, knew where these dividers between worlds were and carefully built their fences along them so that no one passed into them accidentally. The man wrote that,

> ...[the ranch] was rumored to be haunted by evil spirits from the dark world that existed alongside ours. Everyone said that this area where the ranch was located was along an "invisible, thin wall." Which, if one were not careful, they could easily bump into it and fall through the wall into another world! Everyone that I ever spoke with about that wall had the same fear of that other parallel world.[63]

The ranch hand said that he knew an elder tribesman who claimed that if a person were to stand by that "invisible wall" that everything would appear to be of a normal landscape until after a person walked through it. The man then went on to claim that voices could be heard coming from the portal, begging for help, a common skinwalker tactic.

---

[63] Swanson, *The Last Skinwalker: The Avenging Witch Of The Navajo Nation*, p.59.

And strange though it may seem, even the floating balls of light tie into skinwalker lore. In Native American belief systems and Spanish New Mexico folklore both, witches were said to either ride fireballs or turn into fireballs to travel through the air. New Mexico is rife with folktales and allegedly true sightings alike of glowing orbs of light purported to be witches. This, too, applies to the skinwalker in some instances, which is said to be able to turn into an orb of light and fly in some traditions.

So, even though there is that small tie between Southwest witchcraft and lights in the sky, the question still lingers, what is Skinwalker Ranch? Is it simply land cursed by Navajo skinwalkers, or is it perhaps the gateway to another dimension? Forteans for years have spoken of such places, or realms perhaps we should call them. Some call this hidden realm Magonia, others Etheria, but whatever you call it, it seems to lead to an unseen dimension inhabited by monsters and other strange beings. In the words of Jacques Vallée, the Skinwalker Ranch does indeed appear to be a "passport to Magonia."

SKINWALKERS, WEREWOLVES AND HELL HOUNDS OF NORTH AMERICA

Sources:

Kelleher, Colm A. and George Knapp. *Hunt for the Skinwalker.* Pocket Books, 2005.

Skinner, Ryan and Cheryl Lynn Carter. *Digging Into Skinwalker Ranch.* Skinner Enterprises LLC, 2021.

Swanson, Gary and Wendy. *The Last Skinwalker: The Avenging Witch of The Navajo Nation.* By the authors, 2018.

-- *Skinwalker: Guardian of the Last Portal.* By the authors, 2020.

INDEX

Arcadia, 10
Beast of Bray Road, 87, 148, 154
Beast of Gévaudan, 13, 37, 53
berserkers, 14, 111
Bigelow, Robert, 193
Billy the Kid, 55, 208
Bosque Redondo, 55
Bourgot, Pierre, 11-12
Burt, Isabella, 115-119
Cadejo, 45, 129-133
Carson, Kit, 194
Cat People (1942), 107
Chaney Jr., Lon, 14, 115
Cherokee, 27-28
Chickasaw, 30
Chupacabra, 44
Curse of the Werewolf, 16
Detroit, Michigan, 17
Devil's River, 134-142
Dinehtah, 56, 67
Dobie, J. Frank, 86, 155-164
Dog Eater, 39-53, 121, 188
Eldorado Canyon, 72-78
Espontosa Lake, 138
Fort Defiance, Arizona, 67
Fort Sumner, New Mexico, 55
Fort, Charles, 194
Foster, Lance M., 121, 125
Ganado Lake, Arizona, 59, 63, 65
Godfrey, Linda S., 94, 148
Grosse Pointe werewolf, 17-22
Haunted Highway, 77
hellhounds, 70-80, 129-133
Herodotus, 11
Hubbell, Charles, 60-69
Hubble, Juan Lorenzo, 60
Hutchins, Israel, 123
Hutchins, Ross, 123
Ioway tribe, 121
Keel, John, 154, 193
Kentucky Lake, 29
Kirby, Jack, 126
Lake St. Clair, 17-22
Long Walk, 55
loup garou, 16-18
Lycaon, 9-10
Marshall, Robert E., 163
McCurdy, Elmer, 204
Mescalero Apache, 55
Mexico, Missouri, 107-110
Michigan Dogman, 23-26
Morgan, Red, 101-103
Morgan's Raiders, 35-36
Mothman, 193-194
Navajo, 55-69, 194, 198, 201, 203
Navajo Witch Purge, 55-69
onza, 155-164
Parent, Genevieve, 17-18
Raton, New Mexico, 143-146

SKINWALKERS, WEREWOLVES AND HELL HOUNDS OF NORTH AMERICA

Red River Gorge, Kentucky, 27-29
ringdocus, 124, 127
Rock River, Illinois, 149
Rose Hill Cemetery, Idaho, 128
Ruggles, C.B., 156-163
Saskatchewan, Canada, 101
Shimmerhorn, Silas, 35-36
shunka warak'in, 120-127
Skinner, Alanson, 121-123
Skinner, Charles, 18, 20, 22
skinwalkers, 15, 28, 57-58, 64-66, 69, 82-86, 155, 192, 193-195, 198, 201-202
Skinwalker Ranch, 191-203
Springfield Corners, Wisconsin, 89
Talbot County, Georgia, 115-119
Trails to Nature's Mysteries: The Life of a Working Naturalist, 123
Urraca Mesa, 193
Ute, 81, 194
Vallée, Jacques, 193
vampires, 15, 39, 41, 45, 132, 191
Vancouver Island, 105
Versailles, Indiana, 35-38
Vincennes, Indiana, 95-99
vulkodlak, 15
Wahhoo, 165-182, 184
Watrous, New Mexico, 81-86
Weatherly, David, 165, 182
Wolf Man, The, 107, 115-116, 119

ABOUT THE AUTHOR

John LeMay was born and raised in Roswell, NM, the "UFO Capital of the World." He is the author of over 35 books on film and western history such as *Kong Unmade: The Lost Films of Skull Island*, *Tall Tales and Half Truths of Billy the Kid*, and *Roswell USA: Towns That Celebrate UFOs, Lake Monsters, Bigfoot and Other Weirdness*. In addition to non-fiction, he is also the author of the novel *The Noted Desperado Pancho Dumez*. He is also the editor/publisher of *The Lost Films Fanzine* and has written for magazines such as *True West*, *Cinema Retro*, and *Mad Scientist* to name only a few. He is a Past President of the Board of Directors for the Historical Society for Southeast New Mexico and the host of the web series *Roswell's Hidden History*.

THE BICEP BOOKS CATALOGUE

The following titles are available for purchase on Amazon.com, and are available to bookstores at a wholesale discount via Ingram Content Group (ISBNs of available editions listed for this purpose)

THE BIG BOOK OF JAPANESE GIANT MONSTER MOVIES SERIES

The third edition of the book that started it all! Reviews over 100 tokusatsu films between 1954 and 1988. All the Godzilla, Gamera, and Daimajin movies made during the Showa era are covered plus lesser known fare like *Invisible Man vs. The Human Fly* (1957) and *Conflagration* (1975). Softcover (380 pp/5.83" X 8.27") Suggested Retail: $19.99 SBN:978-1-7341546-4-1

This third edition reviews over 75 tokusatsu films between 1989 and 2019. All the Godzilla, Gamera, and Ultraman movies made during the Heisei era are covered plus independent films like *Reigo, King of the Sea Monsters* (2005), *Demeking, the Sea Monster* (2009) and *Attack of the Giant Teacher* (2019)! Softcover (260 pp/5.83" X 8.27") Suggested Retail: $19.99 ISBN: 978-1-7347816-4-9

This second edition of the Rondo Award nominated book covers un-produced scripts like *Bride of Godzilla* (1955), partially shot movies like *Giant Horde Beast Nezura* (1963), and banned films like *Prophecies of Nostradamus* (1974), plus hundreds of other lost productions. Softcover/Hard-cover (470pp. /7" X 10") Suggested Retail: $24.99 (sc)/$39.95(hc)ISBN: 978-1-73 41546-0-3 (hc)

This sequel to *The Lost Films* covers the non-giant monster unmade movie scripts from Japan such as *Frankenstein vs. the Human Vapor* (1963), *After Japan Sinks* (1974-76), plus lost movies like *Fearful Attack of the Flying Saucers* (1956) and *Venus Flytrap* (1968). Hardcover (200 pp/5.83" X 8.27")/Softcover (216 pp/ 5.5" X 8.5") Suggested Retail: $9.99 (sc)/$24.99(hc) ISBN:978-1-7341546 -3-4 (hc)

This companion book to *The Lost Films* charts the development of all the prominent Japanese monster movies including discarded screenplays, story ideas, and deleted scenes. Also includes bios for writers like Shinichi Sekizawa, Niisan Takahashi and many others. Comprehensive script listing and appendices as well. Hardcover/Softcover (370 pp./ 6"X9") Suggested Retail: $16.95(sc)/$34.99(hc)ISBN: 978-1-7341546-5-8 (hc)

Examines the differences between the U.S. and Japanese versions of over 50 different tokusatsu films like *Gojira* (1954)/*Godzilla, King of the Monsters!* (1956), *Gamera* (1965)/ *Gammera, the Invincible* (1966), *Submersion of Japan* (1973)/*Tidal Wave* (1975), and many, many more! Softcover (540 pp./ 6"X9") Suggested Retail: $22.99 ISBN: 978-1-953221-77-3

Examines the differences between the European and Japanese versions of tokusatsu films including the infamous "Cozzilla" colorized version of *Godzilla*, from 1977, plus rarities like *Terremoto 10 Grado*, the Italian cut of *Legend of Dinosaurs*. The book also examines the condensed Champion Matsuri edits of Toho's effects films. Softcover (372 pp./ 6"X9") Suggested Retail: $19.99 ISBN: 978-1-953221-77-3

Throughout the 1960s and 1970s the Italian film industry cranked out over 600 "Spaghetti Westerns" and for every *Fistful of Dollars* were a dozen pale imitations, some of them hilarious. Many of these lesser known Spaghettis are available in bargain bin DVD packs and stream for free online. If ever you've wondered which are worth your time and which aren't, this is the book for you. Softcover (160pp./5.06" X 7.8") Suggested Retail: $9.99

207

THE BICEP BOOKS CATALOGUE

CLASSIC MONSTERS SERIES

Kong Unmade explores unproduced scripts like *King Kong vs. Frankenstein* (1958), unfinished films like *The Lost Island* (1934), and lost movies like *King Kong Appears in Edo* (1938). As a bonus, all the Kong rip-offs like *Konga* (1961) and *Queen Kong* (1976) are reviewed. Hardcover (350 pp/5.83" X 8.27")/Softcover (376 pp/ 5.5" X 8.5") Suggested Retail: $24.99 (hc)/$19.99(sc) ISBN: 978-1-7341546-2-7(hc)

Jaws Unmade explores unproduced scripts like *Jaws 3, People 0* (1979), abandoned ideas like a Quint prequel, and even aborted sequels to Jaws inspired movies like *Orca Part II*. As a bonus, all the Jaws rip-offs like *Grizzly* (1976) and *Tentacles* (1977) are reviewed. Hardcover (316 pp/5.83" X 8.27")/Softcover (340 pp/5.5" X 8.5") Suggested Retail: $29.99 (hc)/$17.95(sc) ISBN: 978-1-7344730-1-8

Classic Monsters Unmade covers lost and unmade films starring Dracula, Frankenstein, the Mummy and more monsters. Reviews unmade scripts like *The Return of Frankenstein* (1934) and *Wolf Man vs. Dracula* (1944). It also examines lost films of the silent era such as *The Werewolf* (1913) and *Drakula's Death* (1923). Softcover/Hardcover(428pp/5.83"X8.27") Suggested Retail: $22.99(sc)/$27.99(hc)ISBN:978-1-953221-85-8(hc)

Volume 2 explores the Hammer era and beyond, from unmade versions of *Brides of Dracula* (called *Disciple of Dracula*) to remakes of *Creature from the Black Lagoon*. Completely unmade films like *Kali: Devil Bride of Dracula* (1975) and *Godzilla vs. Frankenstein* (1964) are covered along with lost completed films like *Batman Fights Dracula* (1967) and *Black the Ripper* (1974). Coming Fall 2021.

NOSTALGIA

Written in the same spirit as *The Big Book of Japanese Giant Monster Movies*, this tome reviews all the classic Universal and Hammer horrors to star Dracula, Frankenstein, the Gillman and the rest along with obscure flicks like *The New Invisible Man* (1958), *Billy the Kid versus Dracula* (1966), *Blackenstein* (1973) and *Legend of the Werewolf* (1974). Softcover (394 pp/5.5" X 8.5") Suggested Retail: $17.95

Written at an intermediate reading level for the kid in all of us, these picture books will take you back to your youth. In the spirit of the old Ian Thorne books are covered *Nabonga* (1944), *White Pongo* (1945) and more! Hardcover/Softcover (44 pp/7.5" X 9.25") Suggested Retail: $17.95(hc)/$9.99(sc) ISBN: 978-1-7341546-9-6 (hc) 978-1-7344730-5-6 (sc)

Written at an intermediate reading level for the kid in all of us, these picture books take you back to your youth. In the spirit of the old Ian Thorne books are covered *The Lost World* (1925), *The Land That Time Forgot* (1975) and more! Hardcover/Softcover (44 pp/7.5" X 9.25") Suggested Retail: $17.95 (hc)/$9.99(sc) ISBN: 978-1-7344730-6-3 (hc) 978-1-7344730-7-0 (sc)

Written at an intermediate reading level for the kid in all of us, these picture books will take you back to your youth. Ian Thorne books are covered *Them!* (1954), *Empire of the Ants* (1977) and more! Hardcover/Softcover (44 pp/7.5" X 9.25") Suggested Retail: $17.95(hc)/$9.99(sc) ISBN: 978-1-7347816-3-2 (hc) 978-1-7347816-2-5 (sc)

THE BICEP BOOKS CATALOGUE

CRYPTOZOOLOGY/COWBOYS & SAURIANS

Cowboys & Saurians: Prehistoric Beasts as Seen by the Pioneers explores dinosaur sightings from the pioneer period via real newspaper reports from the time. Well-known cases like the Tombstone Thunderbird are covered along with more obscure cases like the Crosswicks Monster and more. Softcover (357 pp/5.06" X 7.8") Suggested Retail: $19.95 ISBN: 978-1-7341546-1-0

Cowboys & Saurians: Ice Age zeroes in on snowbound saurians like the Ceratosaurus of the Arctic Circle and a Tyrannosaurus of the Tundra, as well as sightings of Ice Age megafauna like mammoths, glyptodonts, Sarkastodons and Sabertoothed tigers. Tales of a land that time forgot in the Arctic are also covered. Softcover (264 pp/5.06" X 7.8") Suggested Retail: $14.99 ISBN: 978-1-7341546-7-2

Southerners & Saurians takes the series formula of exploring newspaper accounts of monsters in the pioneer period with an eye to the Old South. In addition to dinosaurs are covered Lizardmen, Frogmen, giant leeches and mosquitoes, and the Dingocroc, which might be an alien rather than a prehistoric survivor. Softcover (202 pp/5.06" X 7.8") Suggested Retail: $13.99 ISBN: 978-1-7344730-4-9

Cowboys & Saurians South of the Border explores the saurians of Central and South America, like the Patagonian Plesiosaurus that was really an Iemisch, plus tales of the Neo-Mylodon, a menacing monster from underground called the Minhocao, Glyptodonts, and even Bolivia's three-headed dinosaur! Softcover (412 pp/ 5.06"X7.8") Suggested Retail: $17.95 ISBN: 978-1-953221-73-5

UFOLOGY/THE REAL COWBOYS & ALIENS IN CONJUNCTION WITH ROSWELL BOOKS

The Real Cowboys and Aliens: Early American UFOs explores UFO sightings in the USA between the years 1800-1864. Stories of encounters sometimes involved famous figures in U.S. history such as Lewis and Clark, and Thomas Jefferson. Hardcover (242pp/6" X 9") Softcover (262 pp/5.06" X 7.8") Suggested Retail: $24.99 (hc)/$15.95(sc) ISBN: 978-1-7341546-8-9\(hc)/978-1-7344730-8-7(sc)

The second entry in the series, *Old West UFOs*, covers reports spanning the years 1865-1895. Includes tales of Men in Black, Reptilians, Spring-Heeled Jack, Sasquatch from space, and other alien beings, in addition to the UFOs and airships. Hardcover (276 pp/6" X 9") Softcover (308 pp/5.06" X 7.8") Suggested Retail: $29.95 (hc)/$17.95(sc) ISBN: 978-1-7344730-0-1 (hc)/ 978-1-7344730-2-5 (sc)

The third entry in the series, *The Coming of the Airships*, encompasses a short time frame with an incredibly high concentration of airship sightings between 1896-1899. The famous Aurora, Texas, UFO crash of 1897 is covered in depth along with many others. Hardcover (196 pp/6" X 7.8") Softcover (222 pp/5.06" X 7.8") Suggested Retail: $24.99 (hc)/$15.95(sc) ISBN: 978-1-7347816 -1-8 (hc)/978-1-7347816-0-1(sc)

Early 20th Century UFOs kicks off a new series that investigates UFO sightings of the early 1900s. Includes tales of UFOs sighted over the Titanic as it sank, Nikola Tesla receiving messages from the stars, an alien being found encased in ice, and a possible virus from outer space!Hardcover (196 pp/6" X 9") Softcover (222 pp/5.06" X 7.8") Suggested Retail: $27.99 (hc)/$16.95(sc) ISBN: 978-1-7347816-1-8 (hc)/978-1-73478 16-0-1(sc)

LOST FILMS FANZINE BACK ISSUES

THE LOST FILMS FANZINE VOL.1

ISSUE #1 SPRING 2020 The lost Italian cut of *Legend of Dinosaurs and Monster Birds* called *Terremoto 10 Grado*, plus *Bride of Dr. Phibes* script, *Good Luck! Godzilla*, the King Kong remake that became a car commercial, Bollywood's lost *Jaws* rip-off, Top Ten Best Fan Made Godzilla trailers plus an interview with Scott David Lister. 60 pages. Three variant covers/editions (premium color/basic color/ b&w)

ISSUE #2 SUMMER 2020 How 1935's *The Capture of Tarzan* became 1936's *Tarzan Escapes*, the Orca sequels that weren't, Baragon in Bollywood's *One Million B.C.*, unmade movies, *The Norliss Tapes*, *Superman V: The New Movie*, why there were no *Curse of the Pink Panther* sequels, *Moonlight Mask: The Movie*. 64 pages. Two covers/ editions (basic color/b&w)

ISSUE #3 FALL 2020 Blob sequels both forgotten and unproduced, *Horror of Dracula* uncut, *Frankenstein Meets the Wolfman* and talks, myths of the lost *King Kong* Spider-Pit sequence debunked, the *Carnosaur* novel vs. the movies, *Terror in the Streets* 50th anniversary, *Bride of Godzilla* 55th Unniversary, Lee Powers sketchbook. 100 pages. Two covers/editions (basic color/b&w)

ISSUE #4 WINTER 2020/21 *Diamonds Are Forever's* first draft with Goldfinger, *Disciple of Dracula* into *Brides of Dracula*, *War of the Worlds That Weren't* Part II, *Day the Earth Stood Still II* by Ray Bradbury, *Deathwish 6*, *Atomic War Bride*, *What Am I Doing in the Middle of a Revolution?*, *Spring Dream in the Old Capital* and more. 70 pages. Two covers/editions (basic color/b&w)

THE LOST FILMS FANZINE VOL.2

ISSUE #5 SPRING 2021 The lost films and projects of ape suit performer Charles Gemora, plus *Superman Reborn*, *Teenage Mutant Ninja Turtles IV: The Next Mutation*, *Mikado Zombie*, NBC's *Big Stuffed Dog*, King Ghidorah flies solo, *Grizzly II* reviewed, and *War of the Worlds That Weren't* concludes with a musical. Plus Blu-Ray reviews, news, and letters. 66 pages. Two covers/editions (basic color/ b&w)

ISSUE #6 SUMMER 2021 Peter Sellers *Romance of the Pink Panther*, Akira Kurosawa's *Song of the Horse*, *Kali - Devil Bride of Dracula*, Jack Black as Green Lantern, *Ladybug, Ladybug*, *The Lost Atlantis*, Japan's lost superhero Hiyo Man, and *Lord of Light*, the CIA's covert movie that inspired 2012's *Argo*. Plus news, Blu-Ray reviews, and letters. 72 pages. Two covers/editions (basic color/b&w)

ISSUE #7 FALL 2021 *Hiero's Journey*, Don Bragg in *Tarzan and the Jewels of Opar*, DC's *Lobo* movie, Lee Powers Scrapbook returns, Blake Matthews uncovers *The Big Boss Part II* (1976), Matthew B. Lamont searches for lost Three Stooges, and an ape called Kong in 1927's *Isle of Sunken Gold*. Plus news, and letters. 72 pages. Two covers/editions (basic color /b&w)

ISSUE #8 WINTER 2021/22 The connection between Steve Reeves' unmade third Hercules movie and *Goliath and the Dragon*, *The Iron Man* starring Tom Cruise, Phil Yordan's *King Kong* remake, *The Unearthly Stranger*, Saturday Supercade forgotten cartoon, the 45th anniversary of Luigi Cozzi's "Cozzilla" and *Day the Earth Froze*. Plus news and letters. 72 pages. Two covers/editions (basic color /b&w)

MOVIE MILESTONES BACK ISSUES

MOVIE MILESTONES VOL. 1 — VOL. 2

ISSUE #1 AUGUST 2020 Debut issue celebrating 80 years of *One Million B.C.* (1940), and an early 55th Anniversary for *One Million Years B.C.* (1966). Abandoned ideas, casting changes, and deleted scenes are covered, plus, a mini-B.C. stock-footage filmography and much more! 54 pages. Three collectible covers/editions (premium color/basic color/b&w)

ISSUE #2 OCTOBER 2020 Celebrates the joint 50th Anniversaries of *When Dinosaurs Ruled the Earth* (1970) and *Creatures the World Forgot* (1971). Also includes looks at *Prehistoric Women* (1967), *When Women Had Tails* (1970), and *Caveman* (1981), plus unmade films like *When the World Cracked Open*. 72 pages. Three collectible covers/editions (premium color/basic color/b&w)

ISSUE #3 WINTER 2021 Japanese 'Panic Movies' like *The Last War* (1961), *Submersion of Japan* (1973), and *Bullet Train* (1975) are covered on celebrated author Sakyo Komatsu's 90th birthday. The famous banned Toho film *Prophecies of Nostradamus* (1974) are also covered. 124 pages. Three collectible covers/editions (premium color/basic color/b&w)

ISSUE #4 SPRING 2021 This issue celebrates the joint 60th Anniversaries of *Gorgo*, *Reptilicus* and *Konga* examining unmade sequels like *Reptilicus 2*, and other related lost projects like *Kuru Island* and *The Volcano Monsters*. Also explores the Gorgo, Konga and Reptilicus comic books from Charlton. 72 pages. Three collectible covers/editions (premium color/basic color/b&w)

MOVIE MILESTONES VOL. 2 — VOL. 3 COMING SOON

ISSUE #5 SUMMER 2021 *Godzilla vs. the Sea Monster* gets the spotlight, with an emphasis on its original version *King Kong vs. Ebirah*, plus information on *The King Kong Show* which inspired it, and Jun Fukuda's tangentially related spy series *100 Shot/100 Killed*. 72 pages. Three collectible covers/editions (premium color/basic color/b&w)

ISSUE #6 FALL 2021 Monster Westerns of the 1950s and 1960s are spotlighted in the form of *Teenage Monster*, *The Curse of the Undead*, *Billy the Kid Versus Dracula*, *Jesse James Meets Frankenstein's Daughter*, and Bela Lugosi's unmade *The Ghoul Goes West*. 50 pages. Special Black and White exclusive!

ISSUE #7 WINTER 2022 This issue is all about Amicus's Edgar Rice Burroughs trilogy including *Land That Time Forgot*, *At the Earth's Core*, *People That Time Forgot* plus unmade sequels like *Out of Time's Abyss* or Doug McClure as John Carter of Mars. All this plus *Warlords of Atlantis* and *Arabian Adventure*! 100 pages. Three collectible covers/editions (premium color/basic color/b&w)

ISSUE #8 SPRING 2022 *Godzilla vs. Gigan* turns 50 and this issue is here to celebrate with its many unmade versions, like *Godzilla vs. the Space Monsters* and *Return of King Ghidorah*, plus *The Mysterians* 65th anniversary and *Daigoro vs. Goliath*'s 50th.

AVAILABLE NOW, THE NEW NOVEL FROM JOHN LEMAY

Twenty-six years ago, outlaw Billy the Kid's tombstone was stolen from Fort Sumner, New Mexico. Now it has mysteriously been returned. When teenage brothers Pancho and Dorado Dumez steal it themselves, they get more than they bargained for. Encased inside the tombstone is a map that leads to the Southwest's greatest treasure: The Lost Adams Diggings—a canyon comprised of solid gold. But the brothers aren't the only ones on the treasure's trail. So is bounty hunter Seven McCaw, and along with him comes a modern-day incarnation of the Santa Fe Ring—a secretive organization that once ruled the West. Forced onto the open roads of New Mexico, the brothers must solve the mystery of Billy the Kid's death and find the lost canyon before the Ring does...

Printed in Great Britain
by Amazon